Best Resumes and Letters for Ex-Offenders

Overcoming Barriers to Employment Success Series

Wendy S. Enelow, CCM, MRW, JCTC, CPRW
Ronald L. Krannich, Ph.D.

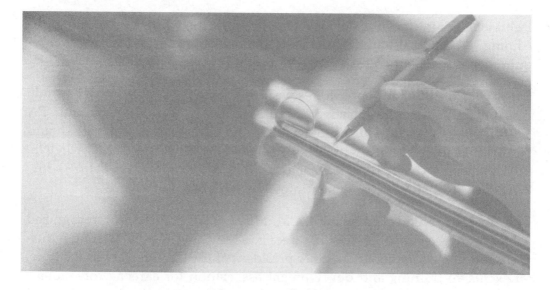

IMPACT PUBLICATIONS
MANASSAS PARK, VA

Best Resumes and Letters for Ex-Offenders

ISBN: 1-57023-251-2

Library of Congress: 2005937741

Publisher: For information on Impact Publications, including current and forthcoming publications, authors, press kits, online bookstore, and submission requirements, visit our website: www.impactpublications.com

Sales/Distribution: All bookstore sales are handled through Impact's trade distributor: National Book Network, 15200 NBN Way, Blue Ridge Summit, PA 17214, Tel. 1-800-462-6420. All other sales and distribution inquiries should be directed to the publisher: Sales Department, IMPACT PUBLICATIONS, 9104 Manassas Drive, Suite N, Manassas Park, VA 20111-5211, Tel. 703-361-7300, Fax 703-335-9486, or email: info@impactpublications.com.

The Authors: Wendy S. Enelow, CCM, MRW, JCTC, CPRW, is a recognized leader in the executive job search, career coaching, and resume writing industries, and is the founder and former president of the Career Masters Institute, an exclusive training and development association for career professionals worldwide. Ronald L. Krannich, Ph.D., is one of America's leading career and travel specialists with more than 3 million books in print. Ron is president of Development Concepts Incorporated, a training, consulting, and publishing firm in Virginia. For more information on the authors, see page 264.

Contents

Acknowledgments

WE WOULD LIKE to extend our appreciation to the following individuals. Without their insights and support, this book would not have been possible. ... To Diana Bailey, Workforce Development and Transition Coordinator for the Correctional Educational Program for the Maryland State Department of Education, and to three members of her team who gave so generously of their time – Elizabeth Crimi and Constance Parker at the Maryland Correctional Institution for Women (MCIW), and Lizz Smith at the Metropolitan Transitional Center (MTC). Ms. Bailey and her team work tirelessly to bring educational programs and services to the ex-offender population through the state of Maryland, preparing them for release and positioning them for job search success.

... To the inmates at MCIW and MTC, we want to thank you for your hospitality, great questions, and wonderful insights into the issues you are facing as you make your transition from prison to the outside workforce. You know who you are and we thank you and wish you the very best of luck today, tomorrow, and in the future.

... And to all of the talented resume writers, career coaches, career transition specialists, and workforce development professionals who contributed their expert resumes and cover letters to this publication. We thank you for your wonderful work and want you to know how greatly we respect you and your contributions to this most unique job search population. You truly are making a difference in the world!

Writing this book was a great experience for both of us and opened our eyes to the complex issues impacting the job search of ex-offenders. Now, more than ever before, we're committed to helping these individuals make successful career transitions, regain control of their lives, and move forward positively and productively.

Wendy Enelow and *Ron Krannich*

Introduction

ONGRATULATIONS! YOU'VE DONE IT! Whether your sentence was six months, six years, or 16 years, you've "done your time" and can now begin to look forward to your new life on the outside. Just imagine waking up each morning, knowing that the day is yours — all yours — to plan and manage how you want, to do what you want, and to be all that you can be. There are no guards to monitor your activities, no regimented schedule by which you have to live, and no doors slamming behind you. Except for parole or probation requirements, you're free to move about as you wish and can now start putting your life back in order.

Making It On the Outside

Before you go any further, take a moment to think about what you've just accomplished and be proud of yourself. What good experiences have you had that will help you make a positive transition to the outside? A prison sentence is no easy task for anyone, no matter the length of time. But, you've done it and done it well, and now it's your chance to put it all behind you and move forward. With the right attitude and motivation, and equipped with critical job search skills, you should be able to make a successful transition into today's workforce.

Along with total freedom comes total responsibility for your life. The thought of that may be a bit overwhelming at this point, but that's to be expected. Change is stressful for everyone, whether it's you, the soon-to-be-released prisoner, a soldier leaving the army for the civilian world, or the 22-year-old college graduate who is striking out on his or her own for the very first time. Everyone in transition sometimes feels overwhelmed; it's a natural response. Realize that and you'll be much better equipped to handle the stress and manage all the changes about to take place in your life.

As you transition to the outside, you face numerous issues in addition to finding a job: food, housing, clothing, transportation, documentation, credit, legal restrictions, and family relationships. However, finding a good job will help you better deal with all of these issues in a more positive manner. In fact, we know that nearly 70 percent of all ex-offenders return to prison within three years. One of the major reasons for doing so is the lack of employment. Getting a steady and well-paying job is the best thing that can happen to you in both the short and long run. It can significantly change your life.

The Book

One of our purposes in writing this book is to make sure you present your best self to employers in order to land a good job that will help you quickly get on with your new life on the outside. This book focuses exclusively on crafting effective resumes and letters for getting job interviews and offers. Hopefully, one or two years from now you will look back and say, *"Using this book for writing effective resumes and letters really helped me make it on the outside!"*

We are well aware of the unique resume challenges faced by ex-offenders as they transition to the work world. Several professionals who work within state and federal prison systems gave us invaluable feedback on resume writing as it relates specifically to ex-offenders. Accordingly, we've incorporated many of their suggestions and insights into this book along with our own work with thousands of individuals facing job and career transitions, including inmates and ex-offenders.

This book is designed for educators, correctional personnel, inmates, and ex-offenders. Many educators and correctional personnel who work with inmates and ex-offenders want a comprehensive resource for addressing the critical writing stages of the job search. They need a resource that is based on sound principles of job search success as well as related to the criminal background and incarceration experiences of their clients. Such a resource must deal with two critical ex-offender issues — red flags in one's background and disclosure of one's criminal history. It also must go beyond traditional resumes and cover letters and include examples of other types of written communications essential to an effective job search. This book does just that.

Communication Skills

At the same time, inmates and ex-offenders also need a resource that will help them better understand the job search process as well as equip them with the necessary skills to effectively communicate their qualifications to prospective employers. Such a resource should include numerous examples of effective resumes and letters that are closely tied to principles of effective job search communication. It should also offer practical advice on how to write, produce, distribute, and follow up resumes and letters.

As you will quickly discover in your job search as well as on the job, employers are especially attracted to individuals who are good communicators. A recent three-year study of 20,000 employees hired by 5,247 managers (by Leadership IQ), for example, found that 46 percent of newly hired employees failed within 18 months. The primary reason for failure was poor interpersonal skills rather than the lack of technical competence. They learned that 26 percent of failures were due to the inability to accept feedback, 23 percent were unable to understand and manage their emotions, 17 percent lacked the motivation to excel, 15 percent had the wrong temperament for the job, and only 11 percent lacked the necessary technical skills. While 82 percent of managers admitted they overlooked poor communication skills in the interview – because they were too focused on other issues, pressed for time, or lacked confidence in their ability to heed the warning signs – many of those communication skills actually surfaced when candidates wrote resumes and letters in their attempt to convey their qualifications to employers.

In the end, finding and keeping a job is all about communication, communication, communication. Accordingly, we designed this book to help you become an excellent communicator at the critical interview screening stage of your job search. Once you get to the face-to-face job interview, you must communicate excellent interpersonal skills in order to get a job offer.

Your Larger Job Search

This book should be used in conjunction with Ron and Caryl Krannich's two more comprehensive job search books designed for ex-offenders – *The Ex-Offender's Job Hunting Guide* and *The Ex-Offender's Quick Job Hunting Guide* (Impact

Publications, 2005). Both books walk ex-offenders through nine other critical steps in the job search process: attitudes, decisions, assessment, objectives, research, applications, networking, interviews, and salary negotiations. Resume and letter writing is the critical seventh step in their 10 steps to job search success. Used with these other books, *Best Resumes and Letters for Ex-Offenders* offers powerful lessons in what you can and should do right in your job search. It helps you **build a new identity** by focusing on what's right about you – your strengths, capabilities, and commitment to living a positive "new" life. Best of all, it gives you **hope** that tomorrow indeed will be a much better day because you have something very positive to offer an employer who trusts you will add value to their operations.

We wish you well as you prepare for today's challenging job market. If you follow the advice in this book, you should be able to substantially improve the strength and quality of your resume, your letters, and all of your other job search communications. In turn, you'll generate more interviews and more offers, and position yourself for career success.

1

What You Need to Know About Resumes

WELCOME TO THE FREE WORLD where you are now entirely responsible for your own future, including your employment success. Whether you are still incarcerated, recently released, or have been out for some time, finding a good job will help put your red flags behind you and change your life for the better, and forever. It will improve your motivation and self-esteem as well as give greater meaning and purpose to your life. It also will give you much-needed cash and benefits for food, housing, transportation, and health care necessary to survive and thrive in the outside world.

Take Responsibility for Your Future

While some employers are reluctant to hire ex-offenders, many others have discovered that ex-offenders are often hard working, honest, dependable, and loyal workers. Your job is to convince employers that you have the right stuff to become a star employee. You'll begin doing this when you start focusing on two key ingredients for conducting a successful job search – writing powerful **resumes and letters** that clearly communicate your qualifications to employers who, in turn, will invite you to job interviews.

Let's be perfectly clear about **responsibilities**. While many people are willing to help ex-offenders find jobs (see our recommended resources in Appendix E), no one owes you a job. And no one is responsible for giving you a job and keeping you on the payroll. You must earn a job based on your **abilities and skills**, and keep it based on your **performance**. But first you must find employers interested in your qualifications and then convince them that you're the "right" candidate. It's not an easy task for anyone, regardless of his or her background. One of the vital keys to locating employers and getting them to invite you to a job interview will be your written communication – your resume and your letters.

Approach It Right

So, you're looking for a job. How do you plan to find a job and communicate your qualifications to employers? Will you just show up at their door and ask for a job? Do you plan to use an employment service to locate employers? Or will you primarily respond to classified ads in the newspapers and on the Internet?

Whatever approach you use, chances are you will need to write a resume, craft letters, and complete application forms. These written documents are keys to finding a job in today's highly competitive job market. Helping you overcome barriers to employment by writing, producing, and distributing outstanding resumes and letters is our major goal in writing this book.

However, writing effective resumes and letters is often easier said than done. For someone with a history of incarceration, the entire job search process is filled with doubts and fears:

- doubts about your abilities
- doubts about how to deal with your criminal history
- doubts about whether or not you'll land a rewarding job
- doubts about being "accepted" on the job
- fear of having to disclose your record
- fear of answering certain questions during a job interview
- fear of being rejected because of your record
- fear of not finding a good job to survive in the outside world

In the following pages we will show you how to eliminate many of these doubts and fears as you go on to find a good job based on much of what you say about yourself in your resume and letters. Use this book wisely and you'll develop powerful writing skills to help you land a great job.

Resume Basics

Welcome to the world of resume writing … a world of keywords, action verbs, accomplishments, job histories, skill sets, technical competencies, and more. It's a world where you can create a resume that is unique to you and your capabilities, and then use that resume to position yourself for a great job, career position, or management opportunity.

Before we can even begin our discussion on resume writing, it is important to understand what a resume is, what its purpose is, and who needs one. So, let's begin with the basics:

Resume: Brief document (one or two pages) that summarizes an individual's work history, training, education, and special skills. Typically used during the job search process to demonstrate qualifications and get interviews. Comprised of three key components:

- **Wording** – what you say and how you say it
- **Format** – chronological (focus on work history) or functional (focus on skills)
- **Design** – what it looks like (typestyle, boldface, italics, lines, boxes, and more)

Purpose of a Resume: To get job interviews. That's it! Resumes, themselves, do NOT get jobs. Only people, like yourself, can do that. The resume is simply the means to an end, the tool that you'll use to communicate your experience, sell your skills, and entice a company to invite you to an interview. Once you're in the door for the interview, the resume can be used as a "talking point," allowing you to describe in more detail the specific information you've included on the resume.

Who Needs a Resume? Everyone. Whether you're looking for a job as a nurse's aide, carpenter, food-service worker, salesperson, or company executive, everyone needs a resume. It's your personal calling card that introduces a prospective employer to your unique set of skills, work experiences, and training.

Now that you have a basic understanding of what a resume is, its purpose, and who needs one, we're going to take it one step further and explore:

- The top 15 things that you must know about a resume
- The top 15 resume writing mistakes to avoid
- The top 15 resume production and distribution mistakes to avoid

Read these sections very carefully, for they include information that is essential to writing and designing powerful resumes that open doors, get you noticed, and help position you for great employment opportunities.

Top 15 Things You Must Know About Resumes

1. **There are no rules for resume writing!** One of the greatest challenges of resume writing is that there are no specific rules about what to write, how to write it, and what to make it look like. There are certain guidelines, of course, such as including your work experience, training, and education. Beyond that, there are no formal rules or standards for how to write a resume, and this can make the process seem difficult and frustrating. But this doesn't mean you can just write anything you want to on a resume. After all, employers have certain expectations as to what should be included on a resume.

    Don't be alarmed! As you read through this book and review all of the sample resumes, you'll be able to determine what type of resume is right for you, how to write it, how to format it, and how to make it look attractive. Feel free to use some of the wording that best represents your talents and select a format that you like from these resumes. Our examples are presented here as tools for you to use in writing and designing your own winning resume. Since your final resume should represent the real you, avoid trying to short-cut this process by just copying our examples.

2. **Resume writing is all about sales.** Suppose, for example, that you work in a clothing store. A new line of clothing has just arrived, and it is your responsibility to put those clothes out on the sales floor, creating merchandise displays that are attractive and encourage shoppers to pick up the new products. Bottom line, sales is always about getting the customer to look closely at a product, evaluate it, and then, hopefully, make the decision to purchase it.

    Well, resume writing is no different! You're the product that's for sale, and it's your responsibility to write and design a resume that is attractive to your buying audience (the companies you want to work for) and makes them look at you closely. Then, hopefully, once they're impressed with the quality of the merchandise (your resume), they will then call you for an interview.

Now, carefully consider what we've just written ... **that resume writing is all about sales** ... and you'll understand how you must "think" about resumes. Your resume is your personal sales tool, and you must effectively "merchandise" your skills, talents, achievements, work history, education, training, technical competencies, and all the other qualifications that you bring to the workforce. Every word that you write on your resume must be carefully considered to be sure that you are "selling" yourself and not just writing a listing of where, when, and what.

3. **Resumes are NOT autobiographies!** All too often job seekers believe that they have to include **everything** about themselves on a resume – every job they've ever had, every class they've ever taken, every computer program they've ever used (even if it's 10 years old!) – everything, even their criminal record. Not true!

Rather, a resume is a snapshot of the **highlights** of your work experience, skills, and educational background. Like good advertising copy, your resume should be designed to move the reader to take action – in this case, entice a prospective employer to call you for an interview. The only information you need to include is information that will help position you for a new job opportunity. Generally, this will include some, if not all, of your work experience, your educational background, and any specialized training or certifications, along with a summary of your skills. The "Skills Summary," which we'll discuss at length later in this book, can be presented in a number of different formats and styles, and is as important to your resume as your work experience and education.

4. **Career Objectives are important.** One controversy in resume writing is whether or not to use an Objective. Some resume writers, recruiters, and career coaches think that they are a must. Others think they are unnecessary. To help you decide whether you need an Objective on your resume, ask yourself these three questions:

A. **Do you have a specific Objective in mind?** A specific position? A specific industry? If so, you can include a focused Objective statement such as: "Seeking an entry-level position in the Telecommunications Industry" or "Payroll Clerk with a major insurance company in the Chicago metro area." As you can see, each of these Objective statements clearly indicates the type of position the individual is seeking along with his or her industry preference. **If you are this focused in your job search, do include an Objective on your resume.**

B.   Is your Objective constant? Will your Objective stay the same for virtually all jobs you apply for and all the resumes you submit? If so, include a focused Objective such as outlined in A above. If not, do not include one. You do not want to have to edit your resume each and every time you send it, adjusting your Objective to fit the position. It's time-consuming and stalls the flow of resumes out your door, unless you have computer access **all** of the time. **Only include an Objective on your resume if your career goals are focused and constant.**

C.   Is your Objective unclear? Are you considering a number of different opportunities? Are you pursuing a number of different jobs? Are you interested in opportunities in many different industries? If your answer is yes, do not include an Objective statement, for it will be unfocused and vague. An Objective statement such as "Seeking a position with an established company offering opportunities for career training and long-term promotion" says nothing! These are useless words and add no value to your resume. They do not tell your reader "who" you are or "what" type of job you are pursuing. **If you are unclear about your Objective, do not include it on your resume.**

Ideally, you should include an Objective on your resume. After all, it gives purpose to your writing and helps structure everything else that appears on the resume. It helps you target your job search toward particular jobs and employers rather than wander aimlessly from one interesting job to another. In addition, it answers one question employers often ask about candidates – *"What does he or she really want to do?"* If it looks like you don't know what you want to do, chances are the employer may think you lack focus and thus you may not stay around very long – you're just looking for any job for the pay and benefits. Best of all, employers appreciate strong Objectives on resumes.

Unfortunately, many candidates write very self-centered, weak, trite, or meaningless Objectives that actually weaken rather than strengthen their resumes. If you are unable to craft a strong and thoughtful employer-centered Objective, you should consider leaving it off of your resume and following our suggested options. But remember, you may appear unfocused and the reader will have to "interpret" from the content of the resume what it is you really want to do. If you are competing with another candidate whose resume includes a strong employer-centered Objective, you may be knocked out of the competition. However, one alternative is to use a Summary instead of an Objective at the beginning of your resume. Written well, a Summary can clearly communicate "who" you are and what type of position you want.

For an extended discussion on formulating Objectives for resumes, including examples of well-crafted employer-centered Objectives for ex-offenders, see Chapter 7 of Ron and Caryl Krannich's companion volume *The Ex-Offender's Job Hunting Guide* (Impact Publications, 2005).

Remember, every time you forward a resume you will also be sending a cover letter. If you choose not to include an Objective on your resume, be sure to state it clearly in each cover letter that you write. This allows you to customize your Objective to each specific situation and each company's needs.

If you choose to include an Objective, here are two samples from which you can select. Or, look through the other samples in this book for different types of wording and other formats for your Objective.

CAREER GOAL: MANAGEMENT TRAINEE with UPS

JOB OBJECTIVE: Entry-level position in Telecommunications Systems Repair where I can apply my strong academic training and practical hands-on experience in systems installation, troubleshooting, maintenance, and repair.

---

5. **Write in the first person (drop the word "I"), not the third person.** When you're writing your resume, you're writing about yourself and, therefore, you should always write in the first person ("I managed product sales throughout the Mid-Atlantic region"). However, resume writing allows you to "break" some of the standard rules of English language and grammar; namely, you can drop the word "I" from the beginning of your sentences so

that your resume reads faster and appears to be more action-oriented and achievement-oriented.

If this seems confusing, take a look at the examples below.

First person – "Coordinated food service for 250 residents."

Third person – "Sam coordinated food service for 250 residents."

Do you see the difference in these two sentences? The first example communicates that "I did this." The "I" that was dropped is understood by the reader. The second example communicates that "Sam, some other guy, did that," and makes it appears as though you were not responsible. Your resume must be a part of who you are and not a distant third-party voice.

6. **Write with action verbs.** Managed, coordinated, supervised, produced, developed, installed, organized, communicated, led, trained, designed ... the list of action verbs is endless and one of the most powerful tools in your resume tool kit. If you write using action verbs, your resume will instantly communicate a message of high energy, action, and results – the message that all employers want to hear about their new employees! Just look at the difference in impact in the two sentences below and you'll understand exactly what we mean.

Writing without action verbs: Responsible for daily supervision of warehouse and loading dock. *(passive and low energy)*

Writing with action verbs: Planned, staffed, budgeted, and supervised daily operation of warehouse and loading dock. *(active and high energy)*

One very important note about action verbs ... they can be used in the present tense (e.g., plan) or the past tense (e.g., planned). If you are currently working, use the present tense when writing that job description. Then, use the past tense for all of your previous positions.

Refer to Appendix B for a detailed listing of action verbs that you can use to develop the content for your resume.

7. **There is no "one-page resume rule."** Have you ever read that resumes **must** be one page long and only one page long? If so, forget it! There is no

limit on the number of pages; however, we strongly recommend that you keep your resume to only one page or two. Any more than two pages, unless a particularly unusual circumstance, is too much information.

Remember, your resume should be designed to entice someone to interview you by sharing the highlights of your work experience, educational background, and skills. If everything fits comfortably on one page, great. If you have enough important information that your resume requires two pages, fine. Just don't allow it to go any further or you run the risk of losing your reader's attention and, therefore, his or her interest in interviewing and potentially hiring you. Indeed, most employers spend fewer than 30 seconds reviewing a single resume – enough time to only glance at a resume. Not surprisingly, the longer the resume, the less likely it will get read.

8. **Use your achievements to sell your success!** Have you ever heard the phrase, "Sell it to me; don't tell it to me"? When you're writing your resume, you want to **focus on what you have accomplished** – your work- and school-related achievements, any honors or awards you've received, your unique skills and talents, and anything else that will demonstrate your potential value to any company that hires you. It is certainly much more interesting for someone to read about what you've learned, contributed, and accomplished than it is to read just a mere listing of the jobs that you've held and your responsibilities. Most important, if you can capture someone's attention with your resume, most likely you'll be offered a job interview and then you're halfway to a new job!

When you focus your resume on your achievements, the entire tone of your resume changes. It becomes more interesting, more informative, and more exciting. See the differences between the two sets of resume statements below and you'll understand what I mean:

*If you **passively tell** about a work-related experience, it might read like this:*

- Worked in a high-volume distribution center sorting packages for next-day delivery.

---

*If you **assertively tell** about a work-related experience, it might read like this:*

- Rated as one of the most efficient package handlers in a 42-person crew, sorting 20-25 more packages per hour than the company's production quota.

*If you **passively tell** about a school-related experience, it might read like this:*

- Attended RTC Technical Institute and earned a Certificate in Computer Network Repair.

---

*If you **assertively sell** a school-related achievement, it might read like this:*

- Graduated in the top 2% of class and awarded a Certificate in Computer Network Repair from RTC Technical Institute.

In summary, one of the most effective things you can do when writing your resume is focus on your achievements – the small ones and the large ones. Most important to remember is that not all achievements have to be astounding (*Saved the company $2 million*). Rather, achievements can be quite small, yet impactful (*Reduced the cost of office supplies by $200 a year*). However, they must be 100% true.

9. **Skills sell.** Not everyone has achievements from their past work experience or education, and that's okay! Just as important to a prospective employer are the skills, qualifications, and talents you bring to their company. In summary, they want to know what you can do and how well you can do it.

    You can present your skills in a variety of different formats and styles on your resume. The two most popular ways are to:

- **Showcase them in a Skills Summary section at the beginning of your resume.** This instantly lets a prospective employer know what you can do for them in one quick glance. Your skills summary might look something like this:

SKILLS SUMMARY:

— Food Service Operations	— Food Preparation & Presentation
— Food Handling & Storage	— Safety & Sanitation Regulations
— Inventory Control	— Customer Service

- **Highlight your skills in your job descriptions**. When you write your job descriptions, always focus on both your **skills and achievements** to let a prospective employer know the value you bring to their organization. When you read the following sentence you can see that this job seeker has communicated her skills in patient intake and assessment, vital signs monitoring, patient transport, and emergency response, all in one quick sentence. Be sure that your job descriptions are rich with skills and qualifications.

> *"Worked with professional nursing staff to coordinate patient intake and assessment, took and recorded vital signs, escorted patients to medical exams, and assisted with emergency response."*

10. **Keywords sell.** Just as important as achievements and skills are when writing your resume, so are keywords – individual words and word phrases that communicate a variety of qualifications. To understand the concept of keywords, consider the words "customer service." When you write those keywords on your resume, you are communicating that you have skills in servicing customers, managing customer relationships, communicating with customers, solving customer problems, handling customer complaints, and more. A single word or two tells a prospective employer a great deal about your skills, experiences, and qualifications.

Keywords are also critically important to your resume for another, entirely different, reason: resume scanning. Many companies scan resumes into their computers before a human eye ever reads them. The computer then actually scans the resume for words and phrases that are required for a specific job. If your resume has those words and phrases, you'll be contacted for an interview. If not, the computer will simply pass over your resume and move onto the next one. As such, you must be sure to put the "right" keywords into your resume – words that not only reflect your skills, but link your skills to the types of positions you are currently pursuing.

Think about that last statement – *"...link your skills to the types of positions you are currently pursuing."* Suppose that you had a career in retail sales before you were incarcerated. While in prison, you worked on a landscaping crew and are now interested in continuing in that field. If that were the case, you would focus your resume on your landscaping skills and not on your skills in retail sales, merchandising, and product display. If, on the other hand, your goal is to return to the retail sales industry, your resume should focus on those experiences and keywords, with only a brief mention of your landscaping skills.

When writing your resume, you always want to write "to the job" that you are seeking. Think about what you've done in the past, think about what you want to do in the future, and then highlight your skills as they relate to your current career objectives. If you can do that in your resume, you will instantly position yourself for job search success. For a great keyword resource, refer to Wendy Enelow's *Best KeyWords for Resumes, Cover Letters, and Interviews* (Impact Publications, 2003).

11. **Using dates can be tricky.** There is a great deal of controversy about whether or not ex-offenders should include dates on their resumes for work experience and education. Unfortunately, the answer is not so simple. There are a number of factors that you will have to consider before you can decide whether putting dates on your resume helps or hinders your job search.

   Here are some general guidelines we've developed to help you determine whether or not you, in your specific situation, should include dates. Remember that these are "general" guidelines, not hard and fast rules, and, as such, you will need to evaluate your particular situation to determine what is in your best interest.

   If you've had a "job" while in prison, then chances are that you'll want to include that job, along with the dates (2002 to Present). This will allow you to demonstrate that you have current work experience and, therefore, minimize the amount of time that you appear unemployed on your resume. (Refer to the next item - #12 – for a discussion of how to present this type of work experience.)

   If you're 50+ years of age, dates become an even more important consideration, even if you have been employed while incarcerated. Be careful not to include dates from the 1960s and 1970s so that you're not "dating" yourself out of the running. You certainly do not want to create the impression that you're "too old" to be a productive and valued employee.

   If you've not had a "job" in prison while incarcerated, then chances are you will not want to include dates of employment on your resume. If you do, your reader will immediately see that you are unemployed, perhaps for as little as one year or maybe for an extended period of time. Either way, we generally recommend in this situation that you do not include dates so you're not instantly leaving the "negative" impression of being unemployed. Companies want to hire people that are currently employed because, in their eyes, it gives the impression of someone who is a reliable worker with employable skills and qualifications. What's more, they often assume that if you're good enough to work for another company, then you're good enough to work for them!

If you do decide to put dates on your resume, here are three of the most commonly used formats:

Years Only   2004 to 2005
(the #1 used format and our most frequent recommendation)

Months and Years   November 2004 to December 2005
(only recommended when your employment experience is very limited)

Duration   5 Years
(effective when you don't want to show actual dates, generally because you have been unemployed for an extended period of time)

Putting dates for your education is also an important consideration for all ex-offenders. If you're going to date your work experience, then most likely you'll also want to date your education. The exceptions to this rule are if the dates are from decades ago or you lack significant education, such as a high school diploma or GED. Again, as with your work experience, you do not want to "date" yourself and appear too old for employment or look as if you lack basic educational qualifications. If, however, you do not date your work experience, then be consistent and omit the dates of your training and education.

Regardless of your age, if training has been the primary focus of what you've done since you've been incarcerated (for example, completed a computer repair training course, graduated from a nursing assistant training program), then you'll definitely want to include those dates. If this is the case, then your education will most likely be a key point on your resume and you'll want to show that it's current.

12. **Do not include negative information on your resume.** If you recall our discussion from item #2 in this section, you'll remember that resume writing is all about sales. You are the product and your challenge is to write a resume that effectively showcases and merchandises that product (you) by highlighting all of your positive attributes (skills, qualifications, technical proficiency, work experience, training). Taking it one step further, you also want to consider the fact that you do not want to include negative information that could be used to immediately exclude you from consideration for a job, such as the fact that you were incarcerated.

Be careful what you disclose on your resume. While you should always tell the truth during your job search, timing is critically important. Being honest does not mean you should prematurely volunteer or confess your negatives or weaknesses on your resume! It is best to disclose the fact that you've been incarcerated at the time of an interview and not on your resume. After all, you can explain red flags in an interview, but red flags on a resume will likely eliminate your chance of ever getting to the interview. Use your resume to highlight the positive and downplay the negative.

Now, with that said, let's take a look at how you can **showcase your work experience from prison without highlighting the fact that it was acquired while you were in prison**.

Using the state in which you were incarcerated as your employer:

Landscape Crew Member – <u>State of Texas</u> – 2002 to Present

Using a company who has a contact with the prison as your employer:

Cook – <u>ARA Food Services</u> – Darlington, SC – 1999 to Present

Using the prison as your employer, but presenting it in a way that makes it appear as though you were employed by the prison itself:

Program Clerk – <u>Jessup State Penitentiary</u> – Jessup, MD – 2000 to Present

In none of the examples above is it obvious that you were an inmate, yet you were 100% honest about your employment during that period of time. Once you are in the interview, you can then disclose the fact that you were incarcerated. Fortunately, at that point, a company is already impressed with your skills and qualifications, or they would not have invited you for an interview. As such, you can more easily explain the circumstances of your incarceration in a one-on-one discussion with your interviewer. This is a much better strategy – and a much more effective way to get hired – then to simply list your term of imprisonment on your resume. If you include your incarceration on your resume, you're giving a prospective employer a reason to immediately exclude you from consideration.

13. **100% accuracy and perfection are the critical standards for resumes.**
Forbidden: typographical, spelling, punctuation, and grammatical errors. Since your resume reflects your best professional effort and thus the quality

of work that you will likely produce for a company, be sure that it's perfect. Nothing less is acceptable.

When you have finished writing and designing your resume, have two or three people proofread it to be sure that you haven't missed anything or made any mistakes. Even though you might proofread it 20 times yourself, it is always better to have another pair or two of eyes review the resume, just to double-check that it is, indeed, perfect. The resume that you submit to a company today is your one and only chance to make an excellent first impression. Don't let a ridiculous typographical error stand in your way!

14. **Do not include salary information on your resume.** Think of your resume as your personal calling card, providing just enough information to a company to interest them in your background, experiences, and skills. It is not the place to discuss salary history (what you've made in the past) or salary requirements (what you want to make now). In fact, research has shown that even when a company asks for salary information in an advertisement, if they are impressed with your qualifications and you have not included that information, they will still contact you for an interview!

The time and place to discuss salary is at the end of a job interview, once you have had the chance to learn more about the position and the company, and once the company has had the chance to meet and get to know you. Then, and only then, is it time to discuss your salary. Although this book is not about salary negotiations, we will share the single most important strategy for negotiating your very best salary – **let the company talk money first!** If you're forced to say a number first, you may have short-changed yourself (you asked for $15 an hour when they had planned to offer you $20 an hour) or put yourself out of the running (you asked for $15 an hour when they planned to pay only $10 an hour). When you let the company talk money first, you then have a specific number from which you can begin to negotiate. For expert advice on salary negotiations, specifically for ex-offenders, please refer to Chapter 12 in our companion job search volume, *The Ex-Offender's Job Hunting Guide* (Impact Publications, 2005).

15. **Do not include references on your resume.** Here's how the job search process works. First, an employer reviews your resume and then, if they are impressed with your skills and experience, they will contact you to schedule an interview. Once you've proceeded successfully through the interview (or, perhaps, several rounds of interviews) and the company is considering making

you an offer of employment, then, and only then, will it be necessary to provide your list of references. When someone is reviewing your resume for the first time, they will not be interested in your references until they have had the opportunity to meet and interview you. Only then, after they are impressed with you, will they be willing to take the time to check out your references and what they have to say about you.

With that said, the time to present references is immediately after an interview. As you're leaving the interview, we recommend that you give your interviewer a single sheet of paper listing your references and their contact information. If your interview has been on the telephone, you can mail or email your list of references (along with a short note thanking that individual for taking the time to interview you and restating your interest in the job). Be sure to include your full name and contact information at the top of the reference list page so your interviewer will know who the references are for!

Top 15 Resume Writing Mistakes to Avoid

In the preceding pages, we've outlined the top 15 things that every job seeker must know about resume writing. Now, we're going to switch gears and focus on the top 15 resume writing mistakes that you must avoid … mistakes that can be the "kiss of death" in anyone's job search.

All too often job seekers submit resumes with serious writing errors, errors that we can almost guarantee will put you out of the running for a job interview. A prospective employer will think to himself, "If this is the quality of work that this individual produces, I certainly don't want them in my organization. I can't have the company sending out work that is confusing and disorganized, with typographical, grammatical, and wording errors!"

To be sure that this doesn't happen to you, avoid the following common errors:

1. Resume is unrelated to the position being filled.
2. Resume is too long or too short.
3. Resume is unattractive with a poorly designed format, small typestyle, and little white space, making it extremely difficult to read.
4. Resume does not include contact information (telephone number, mailing address, email address).
5. Resume is sloppy with handwritten corrections.

6. Resume has misspellings and poor grammar.
7. Resume is wordy and repetitive.
8. Resume has obvious punctuation errors.
9. Resume repeatedly uses the word "I" and, therefore, the job seeker appears overly self-centered and boastful.
10. Resume includes information that seems suspicious and untruthful.
11. Resume lacks credibility and content and includes lots of fluff and canned resume language.
12. Resume is difficult to interpret because of poor organization or lack of focus.
13. Resume uses jargon and abbreviations unknown to the reader.
14. Resume states a strange, unclear, or vague objective.
15. Resume includes distracting personal information that is not necessary to include.

Top 15 Resume Production and Distribution Mistakes to Avoid

After you have written your resume and carefully reviewed it to be sure that you haven't committed any of the 15 critical resume writing mistakes, it's time to move on to the actual typing and distribution of your resume. Again, there are common errors that you can easily avoid if you pay close attention to detail. Here's what you should avoid:

1. Resume is poorly typed and poorly reproduced, making it difficult to read.
2. Resume is printed on odd-sized, poor-quality, or extremely thin or thick paper.
3. Resume is soiled with coffee stains, fingerprints, or ink marks.
4. Resume is sent to the wrong person or department.
5. Resume is mailed, faxed, or emailed to "To Whom It May Concern" or "Dear Sir." (Be smart … call and get a name whenever possible!)
6. Resume is emailed, but the attachment (or pasted-in copy of the resume) is forgotten.
7. Resume is mailed in a tiny envelope that requires the resume to be unfolded and flattened several times.
8. Resume is mailed in an envelope that is double sealed with tape and virtually impossible to open.

9. Back of envelope includes a handwritten note stating that something is missing on the resume, that the phone number has changed, or some other important message.

10. Resume is sent with unnecessary enclosures (e.g., letters of recommendations, transcripts of training) which were not requested.

11. Resume arrives without proper postage and the company has to pay!

12. Resume arrives too late for consideration.

13. Resume arrives without a cover letter.

14. Cover letter repeats exactly what's on the resume, is not interesting, and does not encourage the reader to take action (call you for an interview).

15. Cover letter has typographical, grammatical, and/or punctuation errors and unclear wording.

2

Common Resume Issues, Challenges, and Questions for Ex-Offenders

W E ALL HAVE JOB SEARCH ISSUES, challenges, and questions regardless of our backgrounds. However, ex-offenders have particular concerns because they know many employers may not be interested in hiring someone with both a criminal record and spotty work history. Many of these issues deal with such basics as attitudes, motivations, and goals. Others focus on the mechanics of writing and distributing resumes and letters as well as the unique challenges ex-offenders face given their not-so-hot backgrounds. In addition, many ex-offenders are unfamiliar with how the job market works and how employers hire, from writing resumes and letters and using the Internet to networking and interviewing for jobs. While many of their general job search questions can be easily dealt with by career experts, other questions are more challenging and thus require creative strategies appropriate for people with red flags in their backgrounds.

The Issue of Disclosure

Most job-related questions from ex-offenders relate to red flags that could knock them out of the competition. Indeed, most ex-offenders are especially concerned with the issue of disclosure and how it will affect their job search. They wonder about how to best disclose their crime, conviction, employment time gaps, and incarceration experiences on resumes, letters, and applications as well as during job interviews. We address many of these concerns in this chapter by examining questions we've received from inmates and ex-offenders as they prepare for finding a job on the outside.

Ex-Offender Questions and Expert Advice

During the past few years we have received several letters from ex-offenders inquiring about various job search issues, from legal restrictions on certain jobs, alternative jobs, and resources, to writing resumes and dealing with difficult questions about their backgrounds. Most recently we visited several prisons in the state of Maryland. This gave us the opportunity to share some of our resume and job search knowledge with the inmates. More importantly, the visits allowed us to talk with the inmates and gain a better understanding of the issues they must deal with, the questions they have, and the challenges they face. Although each ex-offender's resume and job search is unique to them and their situation, there are certain challenges every ex-offender must deal with.

The following pages include several important questions we received along with our recommendations on how to best deal with various issues. Common themes running throughout these questions/answers include taking responsibility, developing positive attitudes, keeping motivated, setting goals, and demonstrating performance. Much can be learned about conducting an effective job search by examining this unique set of questions and answers.

Goals and Accomplishments

Question: I can't think of anything I've really accomplished that's worth putting on a resume. The only job I ever had was dealing drugs, which eventually resulted in this dead-end job!

Advice: We all have a history of accomplishments. The problem is recognizing these accomplishments and then communicating them to others in the most positive manner possible. You need to dig deeper into your well of experiences. Think real hard about all of your life experiences – not just a job you held in the past. Think back to when you were a child, a student, a son/daughter, neighbor, church member, or volunteer. Did you belong to the Boy Scouts, Girl Scouts, church choir, a sports team, or participate in some type of volunteer activity? What worthwhile activities have you done while in prison that show self-development and accomplishment? Look carefully at all of these experiences in terms of what you did. What did you do that made you feel especially good about these activities? What type of recognition did you receive? Once you look at these and other experiences, compiled as "short stories," you'll begin seeing patterns of accomplishments that you can include on your resume. For example,

Started a small paper route and built it up to the largest in my district.

Sang tenor in the church choir and was asked to sing solos at several Sunday services.

Earned enough money at Jerry's Diner to help my grandmother buy a much-needed pair of eyeglasses.

Helped a fellow inmate improve his reading and persuaded him to complete his GED, which changed his life.

Most of these "short stories" show a pattern of **taking initiative** and **helping others**. These should be among your many accomplishments that you can reformulate and include on your resume. They also will become important experiences you can talk about during your job interview. These and many other accomplishments are outlined in detail in the self-assessment chapters of our companion book and workbook, *The Ex-Offender's Job Hunting Guide* and *The Ex-Offender's Quick Job Hunting Guide* (Impact Publications, 2005).

Fear of the Unknown

Question: When I leave prison, I'll have nothing – no money, no housing, no job, no car, no tools of my trade, and no family I can trust. Even the tools I used as an electrician were stolen from me by my family that then sold them and disowned me. I'm really scared about what to do once I'm released. I'm afraid I may not make it, especially since I have a long history of substance abuse.

Advice: This is a good reason to start identifying your skills, setting goals, writing a resume, and developing an action plan **before** your release. No one said finding a job would be easy, even for people without a criminal background. While you will face many challenges during your first six months out,

you have within you the power to change your life. Many community-based groups will help you with transitional housing, food, transportation, and job hunting (see Appendix D). If you still have issues relating to substance abuse, which most people in recovery do, be sure to contact one of the many programs sponsored by these groups. Since you already know drugs can ruin your life, keep yourself on a steady road to recovery.

Given your previous experience as an electrician, you should check with the local union about apprenticeships and other programs that can assist ex-offenders in transition. The trade unions in Washington, DC, for example, assist hundreds of ex-offenders in finding good jobs in the construction trades each year.

Be both purposeful and patient in everything you do. Take small but steady steps that will put you on the road to recovery. Your transition will take some time, but if you approach it right, including a positive attitude, you should be able to do well in the long run.

One of the most important things you can do right now is to develop a powerful resume that focuses on your goals and strengths. Spend some time putting together a first-class resume that truly reflects what you do well and enjoy doing. This resume writing exercise will help you focus your life and develop a plan of action that should point you in the right direction for achieving a successful transition despite a few legal and practical obstacles you're facing along the way. It will help you eliminate some of the doubts you have about making it on the outside.

Keep focused on shaping a positive future rather than replaying the negative aspects of your past and speculating about possible failure to move ahead with your life. Remember these words of wisdom as you prepare for your new life on the outside: *"This, too, will pass."* Armed with a powerful resume, motivated with a positive attitude, and focused on putting your transition plan into action, you'll do okay in the challenging months that lie ahead. Twelve months from now you'll look back and say, *"Writing that resume was one of the best things I ever did. It helped me create a clear vision of what I wanted to do and focus on what was important for moving ahead with my life."*

Handling Employment Gaps

Question: What do I do about the long-term employment gaps in my history, both when I was imprisoned and when I was dealing drugs?

Advice: A functional resume is your answer. Functional resumes stress your skills and downplay your actual work experience which is exactly what you need to do in this situation. When you're writing your resume, focus the majority of what you write on the skills and qualifications that you have acquired from any work experience you may have. Also, be sure to highlight additional skills and talents you've learned through any training or educational programs you've attended while in prison.

No Work Experience and Limited Education

Question: I'm 26 years old, have never worked, and only made it through the 8th grade. Should I even bother doing a resume? What skills could I possibly have to highlight in a resume?

Advice: Everyone has skills and qualifications. Sometimes people have acquired them through work experience or training and education. Other times, people have what we refer to as "life skills" … skills that you've acquired through your daily life. These may include things such as the ability to persuade, interpersonal relations (often called "people skills"), organization, time management, budgeting, cash flow management, and more. Use these items and others like them as the foundation for your resume, highlighting the skills and personal talents you bring to a prospective employer.

Lack a Positive Approach

Question: I'm not sure what to do next. I'm an ex-prostitute and drug addict who is still in recovery. I know I have low self-esteem and feel guilty about what I have done in the past. I don't quite know how to forgive myself. But I've tried to better myself in prison and have devoted myself to Christ. I get released in two months, but I'm afraid of what's going to happen next – my family, friends, dating, a job, a place to stay. I can't think of anything I want to do other than be free again. Can you help me?

Advice: Your negative language, which includes "not," "don't," "afraid," and "can't," reflects low self-esteem, lack of motivation, and the absence of a positive plan of action. Although you are not in denial, you've yet to make the transition to accepting the good things about yourself. While you're not ready to write a resume, you've at least taken the first few steps to changing your life – taking responsibility, recognizing some of your weaknesses, and knowing you need to work on your self-esteem. Religion encompasses much more than sin, forgiveness, and redemption. It's also about **hope** – something that you need in order to keep motivated and focused on shaping a positive future. Hope is when you have dreams rather than illusions. Hope is when you take positive steps to change your life. Hope is when you recognize the need to seek help and use that help wisely. Hope is going beyond what's bad about you.

Let's now shift the focus away from your not-so-hot background. Begin focusing on **what's right about you** rather than what's wrong with you. It's okay to forgive yourself and get on with the positive. While you know your weaknesses, do you know your **strengths** – those things that are right about you? In fact, few people really know what they do well and enjoy doing. Once you identify your strengths, your self-esteem will improve considerably. You'll be able to talk about what's good about you and what good you want to do in the future. Best of all, you'll be able to write a resume that focuses on your strengths. There are many tests you can take and several paper-and-pencil exercises you can complete in order to identify your strengths and formulate them into a powerful objective for refocusing your life. We outline several options for doing so in our companion book, *The Ex-Offender's Job Hunting Guide* (Impact Publications, 2005).

Once you've identified your strengths and developed an objective, you'll be ready to write a purposeful resume. After you are released, you'll find numerous community-based organizations willing to help you with everything from transitional housing to rehabilitation and your job search. Given your new-found religious commitments, you may want to seek out several faith-based organizations that are experienced in working with ex-offenders. These organizations are easy to find – just ask your case worker or probation/parole officer for names and addresses – or consult Appendix E in this book for ideas on where you can get such assistance. Many of these organizations have mentors who are willing to help ex-offenders make a positive transition. A mentor can make a big difference in your life. He or she represents hope in its best form — a helping hand to give you a leg up on your road to recovery.

Selecting the Right Resume Format and Content

Question: This is the third time I've been in prison in the past eight years. How can I explain that on my resume and in an interview?

Advice: First of all, our recommendation is that you use a functional resume to focus on the skills and qualifications you have acquired while working in between your prison sentences. In addition, if you've worked while incarcerated or attended any training programs, be sure to also highlight any relevant skills you acquired as a result of those experiences. That way, no one will know that you've been in prison on three separate occasions when they review your resume. During the interview, however, it will be necessary to disclose the fact that you have been incarcerated. We believe the best way to explain this is to say, "I've been incarcerated in three different institutions in the state of Massachusetts over the past eight years. However, during those periods, I have either held a job while in prison or attended various training programs so that I would be certain to use my time wisely."

Resumes vs. Applications

Question: Do I really need a resume since most jobs I'll apply for only require an application?

Advice: More and more employers appreciate receiving a resume in addition to an application form. Here's the issue: an application form requires you to structure information about yourself around questions asked by the employer; resumes allow candidates to showcase their qualifications around their goals and major strengths. Applications favor employers; resumes favor job seekers. Applications also may solicit possible "knock-out" information, such as your criminal background, salary history, and references. This information should be presented at the job interview rather than during the pre-interview application stage. So be very careful in answering such questions on a job application.

You put your best foot forward when you give an employer a resume. Even though an employer may only ask you to complete an application, you will strengthen your candidacy if you attach a copy of your resume to the application. Proactive job seekers write winning resumes; passive job seekers approach prospective employers empty-handed and only ask to complete an application.

A Questionable Employment Experience

Question: I'm in prison because I robbed a fast-food restaurant where I worked. Should I include that job on my resume? I did work there for six months and it's the only experience I have except for a very short-term, part-time job at a hair salon.

Advice: As mentioned in the previous solution, when you are actually interviewing for a position, it will be necessary to disclose the fact that you've been in prison. Since you will be sharing that information in the interview, we recommend that you also include your period of employment with the fast-food restaurant on your resume. By including it, you will be able to highlight the skills you acquired during your six months of employment. Since you do not have a lot of other experience to mention on your resume, this job is important to demonstrate the skills that you do have and the fact that you were a dependable, conscientious, and hard-working employee (despite the fact that you made a poor decision and have now paid the price for it).

Prison Work Experience

Question: Should I include my work experience in prison on my resume?

Advice: The answer to that question is YES! You want to include any and all work experience on your resume so that you can present yourself as a well-qualified employee. Work experience, whether acquired in prison or on the outside, is still experience from which you have acquired skills that will increase your employability and make you attractive to prospective employers.

As you may recall from Chapter 1, although we do recommend you include your work experience while in prison, we do **not** recommend that you indicate – on your resume – that you were incarcerated. There are three distinct ways to present this information on your resume without divulging that you were actually in prison. Although this information is presented in Chapter 1, it bears repeating here:

Using the state in which you were incarcerated as your employer:

Landscape Crew Member – <u>State of Vermont</u> – 2002 to Present

Using a company who has a contract with the prison as your employer:

Cook – <u>ARA Food Services</u> – Darlington, South Carolina – 1999 to Present

Using the prison as your employer, but presenting it in a way that makes it appear as though you were employed by the prison itself:

Program Clerk – <u>Jessup State Penitentiary</u> – Jessup, Maryland – 2000 to Present

Volunteer Activities

Question: Should I include my volunteer activities in prison on my resume? Although it is not a job and I am not paid, I do a lot of janitorial work in my cell block. It gives me something to do with my time and makes me feel productive.

Advice: As with our answer to the previous questions, YES, be sure to include all of your volunteer experience. Whether paid or unpaid, experience allows you to develop skills that you can then showcase on your resume. To present your volunteer experience, you can use one of the three formats shown in the previous solution.

Prison Training Experience

Question: Do you think that the computer training classes I've taken while in prison will really help me get a job? Or, will companies think that just because I did it while in prison, that the programs aren't any good?

Advice: Training, whether in prison or on the outside, is always important to include on your resume. In particular, training that you've received while incarcerated demonstrates to a prospective employer that you used your time wisely while in jail to develop new skills and position yourself for a better job or career. So, as with work experience and volunteer activities that you've participated in while incarcerated, be sure to include all of your training. And, yes, employers will look favorably on the training as long as you can demonstrate the skills and competencies that you have acquired.

Uncertain What to Do

Question: Although I've completed the job readiness program at our prison, I still really do not know what kind of job I want. A lot of different things interest me and I'm having trouble selecting just one possible career path. Do you have any suggestions?

Advice: Our first recommendation would be to continue looking at different types of jobs and career opportunities to see if you can't identify something that most interests and excites you. If possible, ask the career counselor that you're working with at the prison if he or she can recommend other career assessments that you can take that might help you decide what you want to do. You'll find many different tests designed to help individuals identify their interests, skills, and abilities. Some of these tests must be administered by a career professional; others can be completed on your own, with the assistance of a friend or by going online.

Nearly 40 such alternative assessment devices are outlined in Chapter 6 of *The Ex-Offender's Job Hunting Guide.* These instruments work well in helping many individuals identify appropriate job and career alternatives. Some people need to complete several of these tests to better clarify a career path. And still others, especially those with limited work experience, may have difficulty identifying what they do well and enjoy doing.

Most importantly, don't be too hard on yourself. If you haven't worked in a while, it can be very difficult to make career decisions when you're preparing for release. You may find that your best course of action is to be released, take a job that's easy to get and doesn't require a great deal of specialized skill or talent, and then spend a lot of time researching jobs and career opportunities when you're on the outside. You can talk with family, friends, co-workers, and others to learn about other jobs and career opportunities. You can visit a One-Stop Career Center for free assessment assistance. In addition, once you're released, you'll have access to much more information about companies and jobs in the particular area where you will be living.

Lack of Direct Work Experience

Question: What if I have no experience in what I want to do now? Before coming to prison I worked as an accountant, but I won't be able to do that anymore since I was convicted of keeping fraudulent accounting records. While I've been in prison I've completed a training program in nursing and home health care, so that's what I want to do in the future. Since all of my experience is in accounting, do you think that I will even be able to find a job as a nursing assistant?

Advice: There are two "tricks" to writing a resume in this situation. First of all, it is extremely important that your nurse training and certification be the centerpiece of your resume. That is the experience that you want to highlight and draw attention to. In addition, you will also want to highlight all of your transferable skills ... skills that you used in accounting and in business that are just as important in a health care environment. Consider your skills in record keeping and how important they are in documenting each patient's condition, medications, and care procedures. That's what is known as a transferable skill – you can use it in one profession or another. What about your skills in organization, communication, reporting, and more? Think hard about what you did as an accountant; then determine which of those skills would also be important in your new nursing career and be sure to highlight those skills in your resume.

Changing and Keeping Jobs

Question: Is it usual that the first job someone gets when they are released is a long-term job? Or, do people usually get one job and then look for something better ... maybe better pay, better hours, or better working conditions?

Solution: The answer to that question is YES to all of the above! Some people are fortunate enough to land a great job immediately following their release. It might be that they're going back to a job or career that they had in the past, that a family member or friend was able to help them find an opportunity, or that they simply were lucky enough to find a great job with good pay, pleasant co-workers, and a reasonable boss. For others, however, the first job out of prison may very well be a transitional job – one that they will hold for maybe only a few months until they can, indeed, find a better position.

You will have to make that determination for yourself after you've been at your job for a few months when you are better equipped to make the decision about whether that particular job is right for you for the long haul or if you might want to start looking for something else. Everyone in today's workforce, from janitors to company presidents, is always looking for new, better, and more high-paying jobs. Ex-offenders should certainly do the same!

One important word of caution as you venture into the job market for the first time after release. Many ex-offenders lose their jobs within the first 90 days. They do so for several reasons – failure to demonstrate good work habits, engaging in illegal activities, or getting into conflicts with their boss or co-workers. Whatever you do, make sure you present your very best self to employers so that you will have a positive work record when you decide to make a job change. Do what it takes to become an outstanding employee. If you get fired from your first job, you'll add another red flag to your background that will further complicate your life in the free world.

Using Email or the Internet

Question: I've been told that it is critical to include an email address on my resume. Yet, I don't have email and, in fact, have never used email before. Since I'm looking for a job as an automotive mechanic, is an email address really necessary?

Advice: If you have an email address (or will be getting one as soon as you're released), then we strongly recommend that you include it on your resume. The fact of the matter is that many, many people communicate via email now. It's easy and very inexpensive (if not free). However, there are many employers who hire blue-collar employees (such as mechanics), where email is not a regular method of communication and they do not expect you to have an email address. So, let yourself off the hook if this is the type of position you're looking for and don't be concerned about not having an email address. If, however, you're looking for a position in "corporate America," then we do recommend you learn how to use email and sign up for a low-cost or no-cost email service, such as HotMail, Yahoo, and Google.

Your question also raises a larger and much more important issue for ex-offenders concerning the use of the Internet in their job search. Since you've not had access to the Internet while incarcerated, you lack an important information and communication skill that many other job seekers use on a regular basis. Indeed, you may be at a disadvantage because of your lack of Internet skills. Consequently, you need to quickly get up to speed on using the Internet in your job search.

The Internet provides a wealth of information on employment opportunities. It's an especially valuable tool **for researching employers and communicating by email**. If you are not using the Internet, you should do so as soon as possible. You can get free training on, and access to, the Internet through your local library, One-Stop Career Center, and many community-based nonprofit organizations. You can easily set up free email accounts through several major online services, such as Google (http://mail.google.com), MSN (www.hotmail.com) and Yahoo (www.yahoo.com), as well as create special email accounts for managing your job search on several employment websites, such as Monster.com, CareerBuilder.com, and Hotjobs.Yahoo.com.

Community-Based Assistance

Question: When I get out of prison next month, I worry that I won't have anyone to help me with my job search. Are there places where I can get career help for free?

Advice: Many community-based nonprofit and faith-based organizations provide free re-entry assistance. While most of these organizations provide food, clothing, housing, transportation, legal, substance abuse, and mental health assistance, some of them also provide vocational training and job search assistance. Be sure to review examples of such organizations in Appendix D, especially Goodwill Industries, as well as contact your probation or parole officer for recommended resources.

Government also provides free job search assistance to ex-offenders. One of the best resources is your local One-Stop Career Center, run by federal, state, and local government agencies. At these centers, you'll be able to get expert guidance from career coaches, employment counselors, workforce development specialists, and others who are experienced in helping ex-offenders and other individuals with not-so-hot backgrounds find employment. What's more, these centers will generally have computers and printers that you can use to produce resumes, letters, and other materials. In addition, they are also a wonderful source for job listings and employment opportunities. To find the One-Stop Career Center nearest you, be sure to visit the following site on the Internet:

http://www.doleta.gov/usworkforce/onestop/onestopmap.cfm

Contact Information

Question: I don't know what address to include on my resume. Should I use the address of the halfway house where I will be staying for three months or my mother's address, although I certainly do not plan to move in with her once I'm released from the halfway house?

Solution: If you can use the address at the halfway house, that would be our recommendation. If you've prepared yourself well for your job search, you should be able to get a position long before you leave the halfway house. In fact, for many offenders, securing a job is a requirement prior to their release from the halfway house. Once you're working and have moved, you can then notify your employer of your new address. In addition, you'll want to update your resume immediately with your new address and your new job so it will be ready when you need to use it again. You never know when an opportunity may present itself, so we strongly recommend that you always have an updated resume ready at a moment's notice.

Resumes and Portfolios

Question: My career goal is different than most of the other inmates in this facility. I want to work as a fashion designer, graphic artist, or draftsperson so I can use my artistic skills. In fact, I have spent a great deal of time while I've been incarcerated working on my designs and sketches. How can I best present all of these drawings to a prospective employer?

Advice: A portfolio is your answer. Take your very best designs and sketches and put them into a portfolio that you can take to interviews to showcase your work and your talent. In creative positions like fashion design, graphic design, and related careers, a resume is just as important as in other jobs. However, your portfolio is perhaps even more important, allowing an employer to actually "see and feel" what you can do and the talent you would bring to their organization.

Portfolios are also quite valuable to job seekers who want to showcase other talents, achievements, and capabilities. Computer programmers use them to demonstrate their technical abilities, engineers use them to highlight major projects they've worked on, teachers include courses they've developed and awards they've won … the list goes on and on. Regardless of your career objective, if you have information or materials that you want to draw special attention to, a portfolio is a wonderful way to do that.

Attitude and Motivation for Success

Question: The job counselor at our prison keeps telling us that one of the most important things about getting a job once we're paroled is attitude. Do you really think that attitude plays a lot in a company's decision to hire or not?

Advice: Yes!!! Attitude is really everything. It's the basis for one of the most important skills ex-offenders often lack – **self-motivation**. While being incarcerated, many individuals lose hope since no one seems to care, and many develop negative attitudes that affect their motivation to change their lives (why bother?). Once released, they may have negative attitudes and find it difficult to keep positive and motivated in face of so many decisions and challenges that seem beyond their control. Especially during a job search, when you are likely to encounter many rejections, a positive attitude is essential for keeping yourself motivated and focused on your goal – landing a rewarding job you do well and enjoy doing.

Almost any skill can be taught, such as how to operate a piece of equipment, how to manage files and records, or how to post accounting information on a computer. However, attitude is more difficult to teach since it is part of people's motivational patterns. With that said, if you're able to present a positive attitude during an interview and communicate that you're dependable, reliable, conscientious, and a hard worker, a company will often make the decision to hire "the attitude" and train "the skills." Your career counselor is correct; attitude is everything! While you may leave prison or jail with nothing, at least you have an attitude that can change your life. Make sure it's the right attitude for success in the outside world. For information on how ex-offenders can change their attitudes, see the first step to job search success in Chapter 3 of *The Ex-Offender's Job Hunting Guide* or Chapter 4 of *The Ex-Offender's Quick Job Hunting Guide*.

3 Your Two Most Important Resume Decisions

NOW THAT YOU'VE DECIDED to write a resume, what do you need to do next? Where and how do you start?

Before you can even begin to write your resume, there are two critically important decisions that you must make. These decisions will impact **everything** about your resume – what skills, experience, training, and qualifications you include; how you include that information; where you include it; and, why you include it. They are:

> **Decision #1** – What is your career objective? What type or types of jobs are you looking for? In what industries are you most interested in working?

> **Decision #2** – Should you use a chronological or a functional resume to best highlight your skills, experiences, and qualifications based on your current career objective (Decision #1)?

Professional resume writers use this information as the foundation for each resume that they develop. Commonly referred to as "resume strategy," your answers to these questions (your decisions) form the basis for how you will present your qualifications to prospective employer and positively position yourself within the job market.

Now, let's explore each of these issues in detail.

Defining Your Career Objective

To write a truly effective resume, you must have some idea about the type or types of jobs that you will be looking for. Your objective might be very broad (entry-level sales position with a major corporation) or it might be very specific (purchasing management position in the automotive industry). In both situations, however, you have defined the type of position you are interested in and, to some degree, the type of company. Again, your objective can either be somewhat open-ended (position as a cashier or sales associate with a local retail company) or focused (position as an automotive mechanic). Either way, you have clearly identified the "overall" type of position you are interested in, and that gives your resume the "direction" that it needs.

Once you've been able to determine your objective, you will then know precisely what type of information you want to highlight in your resume, how to include it, where to include it, and why. It's that simple! Your objective serves as your guidebook and outlines how you want to "play" the game. For example: If you're looking for an entry-level sales position, you'll want to focus your resume on any skills and experience you have in sales, customer service, communications, order processing, account management, project coordination, problem solving, record keeping, and anything else you can think of from your past that will support your current objective. If, on the other hand, you're looking for a position in purchasing management, then you'll highlight your skills and qualifications in procurement, inventory planning and control, supplier sourcing, supplier negotiations, resource management, supply chain management ... the list goes on and on.

When you have a job objective in mind, the entire writing process is easier and faster. You have a target position (or related types of positions) that you're interested in and you know what to highlight on your resume to make you most attractive to companies who hire for those types of jobs. It really is that straightforward. There are no hidden rules or tricks to the game!

When you write a resume and don't have an objective in mind, it becomes a much more difficult writing process. Your resume can often be considered vague, and it can be difficult to figure out "who" you are. Companies are not going to spend the time figuring out where you might fit into their organizations. It's your job to tell them "who" you are and what you can do, and the only way to do that is by clearly defining your overall objective and targeting the appropriate positions.

Having a career objective in mind when you write your resume is extremely important and will guide your entire writing process. That, however, is an entirely different issue than whether or not you actually include a "Career Objective" on your final resume. That will be addressed in Chapter 4 when we discuss when to use an objective, why you would want to use one, and how to write it.

Selecting a Chronological or Functional Resume

The second, and equally important, decision that you have to make before you can begin to write your resume is which type of resume format will be most effective for you to use – the chronological or the functional. This choice will determine the entire structure, content, and presentation of your resume.

Briefly stated, a chronological resume focuses on your **work experience** while a functional resume focuses on your **skills and qualifications**. Notice that we've used the word "focus" to indicate the primary concentration of each type of resume – the things that are highlighted, emphasized, and showcased. It does not mean, for example, that chronological resumes only include work experience. To the contrary, they also include skills, qualifications, education, and other information that is important to you and your job search. Nor does it mean that functional resumes only include skills and qualifications. Most will also include a brief employment section at the end, along with education, training, and any other information relevant to your current job objective. The real difference between the two lies in the focus, the emphasis, and the concentration of the resume.

To better understand the differences between these two types of resume formats, we'll explore them in greater detail. This information should help you make the decision about which one of these formats is right for you and your particular situation.

Chronological Resume

Definition

A resume that is written and designed to focus primarily on the strength of a job seeker's work experience and related skills, qualifications, and achievements.

Components

Generally, a chronological resume will be have the following components presented in this order:

- Career Objective or Job Objective (optional)
- Brief Skills Summary
- Detailed Work History
- Education and Training

Who Should Use This Resume?

If any of the following apply to you, a chronological resume will probably be your best presentation:

- Strong record of work experience
- Excellent record of on-the-job achievements and contributions
- Progressive work history with steady promotion and advancement to positions of increased responsibility
- Current work experience while you are, or were, incarcerated

Should You Use Dates on a Chronological Resume?

The answer to that question is very complex and depends on a number of factors that are specific to you and your job search. Three of the most important factors are (1) how long it's been since you've held a job, (2) whether or not you've had a job while incarcerated, and (3) how old you are. For detailed information on this topic, refer to item #11 in the list of the "Top 15 Things You Must Know About Resumes" in Chapter 1.

The following resume for Randall Daniels is an excellent example of a chronological resume that focuses on the strength of Randall's work experience as an Electrician's Helper. The resume does begin with a brief summary which highlights Randall's overall skills and capabilities, and then follows with job descriptions that detail his work experience and qualifications. Also note that Randall did include his work experience while incarcerated (Electrician's Helper – State of California).

RANDALL DANIELS

328 N. Grand Avenue, San Diego, CA 99087

555-333-2222 – randan@comcast.net

ELECTRICIAN'S ASSISTANT / ELECTRICIAN'S HELPER

Several years of progressively responsible experience as an Electrician's Helper on both residential and commercial projects. Assist with new installations, repairs, troubleshooting, preventive maintenance, and both routine and emergency inspections. Work with state-of-the-art equipment and technology. Learn quickly, follow directions, and demonstrate initiative. Conscientious and determined.

WORK EXPERIENCE

Electrician's Helper (2003 to Present)
State of California, San Diego, CA
- Assisted electricians with maintaining and repairing electrical equipment and systems at one of the largest state complexes.
- Trained new personnel in basic electrical wiring, installation, and safety procedures.
- Maintain/update work records and reports.

Electrician's Helper (2000 to 2003)
Meyers Electrical Contractors, San Diego, CA
- Assisted with installation, repair, and maintenance of new electrical units and power supplies for residential and commercial systems.
- Read and interpreted blueprints and building specifications.
- Delivered materials to job sites and coordinated inventory control.

Maintenance Work (1999 to 2000)
San Diego Zoo, San Diego, CA
- Assisted with building construction and maintenance projects throughout the complex.
- Hand-crafted wood signs and laid cement pads for visitor areas.
- Installed fencing for animal enclosures.
- Aided emergency response teams.

Sales Associate (1997 to 1999)
Premier Wallcoverings, San Diego, CA
- Quickly learned all facets of wallcoverings business.
- Trained new employees in cleaning, repairs, and patching.
- Balanced cash drawer and daily sales receipts.

Other positions held: Apartment Maintenance Worker, Gas Station Attendant, Route Deliveryman

EDUCATION

San Diego Vocational-Technical Skills Center, San Diego, CA
Graduate, Electrician's Helper Training & Certification Program, 2000

Diploma, Palmer High School, Davenport, IA

Functional Resume

Definition

A resume that is written and designed to focus primarily on the strength of a job seeker's skills, qualifications, talents, and competencies, with a minimum emphasis on work history.

Components

Generally, a functional resume will have the following components presented in this order:

- Career Objective or Job Objective (optional)
- Detailed Skills Summary
- Brief Listing of Work History
- Education and Training

Work History and Education might be flipped in the opposite order depending on which is most important to your current career goals. Always place the most important one first.

Who Should Use a Functional Resume?

If any of the following apply to you, a functional resume will probably be your best presentation:

- Lengthy periods of unemployment throughout your working life
- Lengthy period of time since you've held a position (generally because you've either been incarcerated for an extended period of time or, while on the outside, you were engaged full-time in illegal activities)
- A work history filled with many short-term jobs
- Past work experience that is totally unrelated to your current career goals
- No work history at all

Should You Use Dates on a Functional Resume?

The answer to that question is very complex and depends on a number of factors that are specific to you and your job search. Three of the most important factors are (1) how long it's been since you've held a job, (2) whether or not you had a job while incarcerated, and (3) how old you are. For detailed information on this topic, refer to item #11 in the list of the "Top 15 Things You Must Know About Resumes" in Chapter 1.

The following resume for Tyrone Lawrence is an excellent example of a functional resume that focuses on the strength of Tyrone's culinary skills and experience, with only a brief mention of his work history. Also note that Tyrone did include his work experience while incarcerated (Kitchen Worker — State of Maryland).

TYRONE LAWRENCE

29 Pickard Street ⚔ Baltimore, MD 21229
410-555-9999

OBJECTIVE

RESTAURANT COOK

To assist a restaurant in attracting and retaining a strong customer base, by applying a *passion for the culinary arts* and a *delight for fine food from around the world.*

PERSONAL PROFILE

☑ Experience working in a kitchen environment, filling orders, and developing menu items.

☑ Ability to get the job done by employing critical thinking and problem resolution skills.

☑ Work well as a *team player* and independently with *very little supervision.*

☑ Received commendations for dependability and strong work ethic.

COOKING SKILLS

☑ Prepared a selection of entrees, vegetables, desserts, and refreshments.

☑ Cleaned the grill, food preparation surfaces, counters, and floors.

☑ Met high-quality standards for food preparation, service, and safety.

☑ Trained and supervised workers.

☑ Maintained inventory logs and placed orders to replenish stocks of tableware, linens, paper, cleaning
 supplies, cooking utensils, food, and beverages.

☑ Received and checked the content of deliveries and evaluated the quality of meats, poultry, fish,
 vegetables, and baked goods.

☑ Oversaw food preparation and cooking.

RESTAURANT EXPERIENCE

Kitchen Worker — State of Maryland, Jessup, MD
Short Order Cook — Dino's Restaurant & Grill, Baltimore, MD
Prep Cook/Laborer — Chauncey's Diner, Baltimore, MD
Lunch and Dinner Cook — Paolo's Restaurant, Ellicott City, MD

TRAINING & EDUCATION

Graduate, Culinary Arts Training Course, Catonsville Community College

4

Writing Your Resume: Step By Step

WRITING YOUR RESUME would be so easy if we could just give you a standard outline or template. All you would need to do is answer the questions, fill in the blanks, and your resume would be ready. Not much time, not much serious thought, and no tremendous effort. Life would be great!

Unfortunately, as you already know, that is not the case. Each resume must be custom-written to sell each job seeker's individual talents, skills, qualifications, experience, education, training, achievements, technical skills, and more. Resumes are **not** standardized, they are **not** prescribed, and there is **no** specific formula.

On the one hand, this gives you tremendous flexibility in what you choose to include and how you include it. On the other hand, the fact that there are no rules for resume writing is what can make it such a difficult task. There is no single road map to follow, nor a "one-size-fits-all" strategy. Each resume is unique to each individual.

Further complicating the resume writing process is that fact that most people do not understand that a resume is a sales and marketing document. A resume is **not** a career biography, personal diary, or an obituary to be sent to a friend or loved one. It's critical that you understand that distinction. Your resume is your calling card – an advertisement which should result in getting your foot in the door for a job interview. While it won't get a job, it must be written to **sell** you for a job interview which, in turn, results in a job offer. Therefore, your resume should not simply list where you worked and what training you have completed. Rather, your strategy must be to showcase the "best" of your work, training, and skills so that you can create a resume that clearly communicates, *"This is who I am"* and *"This is the value I bring to your company."* It should clearly and consistently reveal a pattern that tells the reader what you (1) have done, (2) can do, and (3) will do in the future.

You must also realize that writing your resume is not a two- to three-hour task. Most likely, it will take days and days of thought, writing, editing, and hard work. Invest the time that is necessary to build a resume that really does sell you and what you've done – in school, at work, and while incarcerated. If you can do this, you will see a remarkable increase in the number of responses and interviews you'll get. The stronger your resume, the stronger your performance in the job market!

Now that we have established that resumes are individualized documents that can vary dramatically in their structure, format, tone, and presentation, it is also important to note that resumes do share certain common features. Most resumes for ex-offenders will have a minimum of three sections – Skills Summary, Employment Experience, and Training/Education. Some resumes may also have a Career Objective (depending on how certain you are about your career goals). And, finally, there are numerous other sections that you may want to include on your resume depending how relevant they are to you and your background. These sections might include Technical Skills, Volunteer Experience, Honors and Awards, Memberships, and Personal Information.

To help you better understand the structure and function of these resume sections, a short but comprehensive discussion of each follows. Use the information below to help you determine (1) if you need to include a particular section in your resume and (2) what style and format to use for that particular section.

Career Objectives

If you recall our discussion in Chapter 1 (item #4 in "The Top 15 Things You Must Know About Resumes"), we stressed the importance of knowing what your Career Objective is **before** you even begin to write your resume. Your Objective gives you a target and guides you in determining what information to include in your resume and why. We also mentioned in Chapter 1 that knowing your Objective is an entirely different issue than deciding whether or not to use an Objective statement on your resume.

In fact, the use or omission of an Objective is one of the greatest controversies in resume writing. Some professional resume writers and career coaches use Objectives all the time; others, never use them. To help you decide whether a Career Objective section on your resume is right for you, ask yourself these three questions:

1. **Do you have a specific Objective in mind?** A specific position? A specific industry? If so, you can include a focused Objective statement such as: "Seeking an entry-level position in the transportation industry" or "Carpentry position with a residential builder/developer." As you can see, each of these Objective statements clearly indicates the type of position the individual is seeking along with his industry preference. **If you are this focused in your job search, do include a Career Objective on your resume.**

2. **Is your Objective constant?** Will your Objective stay the same for most of the positions for which you apply? If so, include a focused Objective such as that outlined in #1 above. If not, do not include one. You do not want to have to change your resume each and every time you send it, adjusting your Objective to fit the position. It's a time-consuming process and will slow your ability to get resumes out the door and apply for various jobs unless you have immediate access to a computer. But keep in mind the implication of not having a consistent Objective – you probably don't know what you want to do and thus may appear uncertain; you also let the reader "interpret" what you want to do. **Only include a Career Objective on your resume if your career goals are focused and constant.**

3. **Is your Objective unclear?** Are you considering a number of different types of jobs? Are you interested in positions in many different industries? If your answer is yes, do not include an Objective, for it will be unfocused and vague. Consider an Objective worded like this: "Seeking a position where I can help a company achieve revenues and profits." Doesn't everyone want to help a company make money? These are useless words and add no value to your resume. They do not tell your reader "who" you are or "what" type of job you are interested in. **If you are unclear about your Objective, do not include it on your resume.**

Remember, every time you forward a resume you will also be sending a cover letter. (See Chapters 7 and 8 for detailed information on writing cover letters.) If you do not include a formal Objective statement on your resume, be sure to state it clearly in each cover letter that you write. This allows you to customize your Objective to each specific job that you apply for and that company's particular needs.

If you choose to include a Career Objective on your resume, here are a few sample formats you can select from. Or, look through the samples in this book for other formats and ideas.

OBJECTIVE:

Entry-level business position using my strong clerical and administrative skills.

CAREER OBJECTIVE:

Entry-level position in the computer Industry where I can apply my training and hands-on experience in systems installation, maintenance, and repair.

CAREER GOAL: SALES MANAGEMENT TRAINEE

If you don't like the words "Career Objective" for this section on your resume, there are many other titles that you can select from. Take your pick from the list that follows:

- Job Objective
- Career Goal
- Objective
- Career Target
- Job Target
- Professional Objective

Skills Summaries

Resumes are most powerful and most useful when they effectively highlight your skills as they relate to your current Career Objective. In fact, before you even begin to write your resume, you should devote some time and effort to identifying the skills and qualifications you have that are of most value in the workplace. Then, use those skills as the foundation for your resume. They are your greatest selling points and what we refer to as the items you want to "merchandise" on your resume – the information you want to showcase.

There are many different ways to draw attention to your skills in your resume. They can be included in your job descriptions, highlighted with your training, or inserted as a separate section at the beginning of your resume (immediately following your Career Objective if you have chosen to include one on your resume).

Writing a Skills Summary at the beginning of your resume allows you to quickly communicate your value to a potential employer. With one quick glance, someone can instantly see the skills and qualifications that you offer and, hopefully, make the determination that you would be a valuable asset to their company and offer you the opportunity for a personal interview.

Following are several sample Skills Summary sections used by ex-offenders to help position themselves for new jobs and career opportunities. Review each of the examples carefully so that you'll understand how they were used and why they were written the way that they were.

HEADLINE FORMAT

(Quick, easy-to-read presentation that clearly defines job seeker's skills and current career goal; best used with a chronological resume)

TRUCK DRIVER – **Flat Beds & Dump Trucks**
Class A & Class B Commercial Driver's
  License Endorsements: PTX
Passenger – Double/Triple Trailers – Hazmat Vehicles
Perfect Driving Record

TECHNICAL SKILLS FORMAT

(Quickly summarizes and presents specific technical skills and qualifications; best used with a chronological resume)

CERTIFIED SURVEY TECHNICIAN

Surveying Instruments:	Electronic Total Station Equipment (Wild T-1000, Sokkia Set 5A)
	Engineers' Steel Tapes
	Plumb Bobs
	Level (to obtain elevations)
Technical Skills:	CAD (Computer-Added Design)
	Blueprint Reading & Interpretation
High Rate of Precision:	Average Error of Closure 1:45,000

NARRATIVE FORMAT

(Provides comprehensive career overview with emphasis on core skills and competencies, in addition to specific career highlights/programs/projects; for use with a chronological or functional resume)

CAREER SUMMARY:

Teacher/Counselor of youth and adults, dedicated to overcoming their obstacles to learning and instilling in them the skills necessary to be productive members of society. Outstanding ability to relate student needs and increase their motivation to succeed. Major strength in organizing resources and participants for special programs.

Populations Served: High-school dropouts or adult returnees of all ages; parolees; the homeless, unskilled, unemployed, and mentally impaired; and recovering alcoholics and substance abusers.

Areas of Effectiveness:
- High school diploma/GED preparation
- High school proficiency testing/academic assessment
- Basic skills and adult life skills instruction
- Career exploration/aptitude testing
- Crisis intervention

QUALIFICATIONS FORMAT

(Summarizes a lot of information very quickly and brings attention to the highlights of training and/or work experience; can be used with a chronological or functional resume)

CERTIFIED NURSE'S AIDE

- Completed CNA Program with honors.
- Delivered over 200 hours of direct, hands-on patient care.
- Skilled in taking vital signs, providing routine and emergency care, and transporting patients.
- Strong and energetic with good interpersonal skills.
- Intelligent and committed; worked as literacy volunteer and tutor.
- Fast learner; eager to develop new skills and competencies.
- PC proficient with Word, Excel, Access, and PowerPoint.

EXPERIENCE SUMMARY FORMAT

(Brings all of the job seeker's core skills, qualifications, and experience to the forefront to downplay unstable record of work experience; best used with a functional resume)

EXPERIENCE SUMMARY:

Offering 15 years of experience in electronic assembly and machining. Proficient in sub and final assembly, test, and inspection of electronic and automotive components, including printed circuit boards, wiring, and other products.

Electronic Assembly/Machining

Assembled and built printed circuit boards and automotive parts (exhaust and intake for Ford cars) from blueprints and schematics using soldering irons, gauges, and various other hand tools.

Operated exhaust machine and made minor repairs/adjustments to computer to maintain production goals and minimize downtime.

Quality Control / Shipping & Receiving

- Inspected over 300 boxes of electronic parts each day to ensure compliance with company standards.
- Recorded incoming and outgoing shipments; verified information against bills of lading, invoices, orders, and other company records.

Team Leadership

- Selected by management as lead person on Xtel product line; oversaw team of 15 assemblers.
- Provided training, guidance, and ongoing support to assembly team members to achieve company productivity goals.

SKILLS OVERVIEW FORMAT

(Positions job seeker for a number of different types of job opportunities when uncertain about career objective and has a minimum of work experience; best used with a functional resume)

SUMMARY OF CAPABILITIES

Prep Cook * General Laborer * Janitor * Barber * Machine Operator

- Responsible, easygoing individual. Focus on being a positive force in the workplace. Persistent and persevering in approach to achieving goals.

- Work capably and skillfully with hands as well as with hand tools or machines to perform job. Quality-conscious.

- Understand and carefully follow instructions. Logical, objective approach to problem solving. Adhere to all company policies.

- Dependable and steady team member. People-oriented; build good relationships. Work well with people from diverse backgrounds and cultures.

- Skilled in the use of a variety of machines and equipment, including:

Steel industry machinery	Boring machine	Lay machine
Stitching machine	Paint & dye machine	Presser
Packaging equipment	Landscaping tools	Hair care
Floor care equipment	Commercial dishwasher	Painting tools

If you don't like the words "Skills Summary" for this section on your resume, there are many other titles that you can select from. Take your pick from the list that follows:

Skills Profile	Qualifications Summary	Qualifications
Career Achievements	Technical Competencies	Experience Summary
Career Summary	Career Highlights	Value Offered

Employment Experience

Writing the Employment Experience section of your resume may take you more time than any of the other sections, particularly if you've chosen the chronological style as your best resume format. With a chronological resume, your job descriptions are the real substance of your resume, and you must spend adequate time to develop them effectively. On the other hand, if you've chosen to use a functional resume, where the greatest emphasis is on your skills and not your work experience, then the Employment Experience section of your resume will be brief and easy to write.

Let's explore the differences in Employment Experience sections on a chronological versus functional resume in more detail. (NOTE: If you're still not sure which type of resume you want to use – chronological or functional – please re-read Chapter 3 where this topic is explored in detail.)

When using a chronological resume, your job descriptions are critically important to the strength and effectiveness of your resume. It is in the Employment Experience section where you'll include your work history (job titles and employers), along with strong and solid descriptions of what you did in each of those positions and how well you did it. Your goal is to write job descriptions that are brief, yet comprehensive, and include your job responsibilities, achievements, project highlights, promotions, awards, work-related skills, and any other important information.

Whether or not you choose to include dates of employment on your resume will depend on your specific situation. For more information on when to use dates and when not to use dates, refer to item #11 in the "Top 15 Things You Must Know About Resumes" in Chapter 1.

Following are some sample formats that you may want to consider for your Employment Experience section if you are using a chronological resume.

ACHIEVEMENT FORMAT

(Best strategy for showcasing work-related achievements; recommended for a chronological resume)

CAREER HIGHLIGHTS

Sales Manager   5 Years
REYNOLDS BOATING SALES & SERVICE, Nags Head, NC

Recruited to improve sales volume and increase profitability of locally owned boat sales and service company featuring eight lines of boats ranging in price from $15,000 to $100,000+. Delivered strong and sustainable growth and financial contributions:

Achievements:

- Drove sales from 40 units ($800,000 in monthly revenue) to 60 units ($1.3 million in monthly revenue) by instituting formal selling procedures and training sales personnel.
- Upgraded finance department's capabilities with new technology and recruited/trained new finance manager with extensive credit and lending experience.
- Created the first-ever documentation process for the company to chart both unit sales and revenues, and provide year-to-date comparisons.
- Won the 2004 "Salesman of the Year" award from Monterey Boats for highest sales volume of any associate in the U.S.

PROJECT HIGHLIGHTS FORMAT

(Excellent format for highlighting specific projects and special assignments as part of your job responsibilities; recommended for a chronological resume)

WORK EXPERIENCE AND PROJECT HIGHLIGHTS:

NETWORK SYSTEMS ENGINEER – Ryerson Systems – Duluth, MN
Traveled throughout the state of Minnesota to coordinate the installation, maintenance, repair, and upgrade of network systems for commercial clients in the transportation, logistics, warehousing, and supply chain management industries. Worked independently with little or no direct supervision. Highlights:

Dove Creek Installation – Coordinated the installation of a $2.1 million local area network (LAN) for one of the area's major real estate developers. Networked 16 different locations with minimal disruption to daily workflow.

Lewis & Brothers Upgrade – Responded to customer needs with the design and installation of an upgraded wide area network (WAN) to manage information flow between various company locations nationwide. Completed project on time and $10,000 under budget.

Lion Iron Works Maintenance Program – Designed and implemented a 24/7 maintenance system to monitor the operations of on-site network supporting 2,000+ users on a 150-acre industrial complex. Managed the entire project from start to finish with no input from management team.

Team Training & Support – Selected from a staff of more than 20 eligible individuals to lead field training and orientation for newly hired technicians. Trained over 15 individuals over two years.

FUNCTIONAL FORMAT

(Effective for highlighting a number of different skills and areas of responsibility within a particular job; recommended for a chronological resume)

EMPLOYMENT EXPERIENCE:

Health Care Clerk, Lexican Health Care, Missoula, MT   Present
Employed with the area's largest health care system (25,000+ patient visits annually). Responsible for a broad range of daily activities:

Patient Relations: Act as receptionist, greeting patients, answering questions, researching information, and scheduling appointments.

Records Management: Maintain patient confidentiality and accuracy in updating charts and files. Ensure strict adherence to all local, state, and federal guidelines and regulations (including HIPAA).

Inventory Control: Monitor inventory of all medical equipment, supplies, and disposable products. Contact vendors to place orders, and review orders upon receipt.

Physician Assisting: Prepare examination rooms and equipment for patients; assist doctors in administering health care treatments, procedures, and medications.

(NOTE: The above job description was written for an individual who was incarcerated and worked for a prison contractor – Lexican Health Care – during her imprisonment.)

EXPERIENCE SUMMARY FORMAT

(Best used when you've had a number of similar positions and you want to include only brief job descriptions; recommended for a chronological resume)

EXPERIENCE

LIBRARY ASSISTANT, Ohio State University, Toledo, Ohio   2000 to Present
Work with full-time permanent staff to introduce and manage policies, programs, and circulation of more than 10,000 items annually. Shelve books, research publications, and assist with upgrading PC technology.

LIBRARY ASSISTANT, Monarch Health Care, Sims, Ohio   1998 to 2000
Assisted doctors and medical students in conducting research, finding materials, and compiling data for reports. Checked materials in and out.

RESOURCE AIDE, State of Ohio, Ada, Ohio   1996 to 1998
Assisted patrons with locating reading and resource materials from card catalog. Reshelved books, periodicals, videos, and audio tapes.

(NOTE: The "Resource Aide" position above was during this individual's incarceration.)

Now, let's transition to a discussion of functional resumes where skills are the foundation and the most important components. If you decide to use a functional resume, your Employment Experience section will be brief — generally only a quick listing of job titles and employers. The vast majority of your skills and experiences will have already been summarized in the Skills Summary section of your resume.

Whether or not you choose to include dates of employment on your resume will depend on your specific situation. For more information on when to use dates and when to exclude dates, refer to item #11 in the "Top 15 Things You Must Know About Resumes" in Chapter 1.

Following are some sample formats that you may want to consider for your Employment Experience section if you are using a functional resume.

EMPLOYMENT LISTING FORMAT

(Best used in a functional resume where skills, experiences, and qualifications are explained in detail in the Skills Summary section)

WORK HISTORY:

Janitor, State of Texas Department of Public Safety – San Antonio, TX
Assembler/General Laborer, Dirksen Iron Works, Inc. – Austin, TX
Security Guard, Dyson Electronics, Inc. – Austin, TX
General Laborer, Barnes Construction Services – San Antonio, TX
General Laborer, Tidwell Construction – San Angelo, TX

(NOTE: The "Janitor" job above was during this individual's incarceration.)

EMPLOYMENT SUMMARY FORMAT

(Allows you to include very brief information about each position; best used in a functional resume)

EMPLOYMENT HISTORY:

State of Idaho, Boise, Idaho (2002 to Present)

Maintenance Supervisor

Promoted from Maintenance Mechanic to Maintenance Supervisor within 16 months of hire. Demonstrated excellent maintenance, record keeping, training, and supervisory skills.

Belcamp Industries, Inc., Boise, Idaho (1999 to 2000)

Maintenance Engineer

Promoted rapidly through several responsible positions with one of the area's largest electronics manufacturers. Won three "Perfect Attendance" awards.

If you don't like the words "Employment Experience" for this section on your resume, there are many other titles that you can choose. Take your pick from the list that follows:

Employment History	Work Experience	Job Experience
Career History	Career Experience	Job History
Employment Chronology	Professional Experience	Career Path

Training and Education

Writing the Training and Education section on your resume should be relatively easy. There is generally not any real "writing" involved; it's more a decision of where to include the information and how to visually present it. The single most important question that you'll have to ask yourself is, "How related to my current career goals is my training and education?" This question is important because it will determine where you should place the education section on your resume.

Some resumes begin with an Objective, followed by the Skills Summary, then Education, and then Employment Experience. This is recommended if your training and education support your current career goals more than your past work experience. For example, if you've just completed a computer training program in prison and are now looking for a position in the computer field, then include your Education immediately after your Skills Summary.

On the flip side are individuals whose work experience best supports their current career goals. If you're one of these people, then the order of information on your resume will be Objective, Skills Summary, Employment Experience, and then Education. For example, perhaps you worked as a salesperson prior to your prison sentence, and you now want to return to sales. Obviously, your work experience is more in line with your current career goals, so be sure to include your Employment Experience immediately after your Skills Summary.

Once you've determined where you're going to place the Education section on your resume, you can then choose from one of the following formats. Be sure that you select the format that is right for you and your particular qualifications.

COLLEGE DEGREE FORMAT

(Emphasizes college degrees and academic performance; can be used with either a chronological or a functional resume format)

EDUCATION:

B.S., Finance, Magna Cum Laude, University of Missouri, 2001
A.A., Accounting, Honors Graduate, Piedmont Community College, 1998

COLLEGE CAREER FORMAT

(Highlights college attendance – no degree – and other training; can be used with either a chronological or a functional resume format)

TRAINING AND EDUCATION

Business Major	Milwaukee City College	1 year
Business Major	Iron City Community College	2 years
General Studies	Palomar Community College	1 year
Computer Training	Devry Technical Institute	6 mos.
Communication Skills	Palomar Community College	3 mos.
Graduate	Dunbar High School	4 years

COURSE HIGHLIGHTS FORMAT

(Best used to highlight specific coursework; can be used with either a chronological or a functional resume)

FORMAL ACADEMIC TRAINING:

Johnstown Community College – Johnstown, PA – 1998-2001

Social Services Curriculum:

Abnormal Psychology, Chemical Dependency, Case Management, Counseling, Child Psychology, Adolescent Psychology, Social Work Theory, Statistics

ReMark Corporation – Latrobe, PA – 1997-1998

Formal Training Courses:

Personnel Training, Performance Evaluations, Personnel Record Keeping, Safety & Regulatory Compliance, Corporate Reporting

---

TECHNICAL TRAINING FORMAT

(Emphasizes technical training, degrees, and/or certifications; can be used with either a chronological or a functional resume format)

TECHNICAL TRAINING:

Certificate in PC Maintenance & Repair, 2004
DEVRY INSTITUTE OF TECHNOLOGY, Altamonte, CA

Certificate in Computer Programming, 2000
SAM JONES COMMUNITY COLLEGE, Santa Ana, CA

High School Graduate (Computer Science Program), 1999
SANTA ANA HIGH SCHOOL, Santa Ana, CA

CERTIFICATION FORMAT

(Emphasizes certifications and/or licenses; can be used with either a chronological or a functional resume format)

EDUCATIONAL CREDENTIALS

Medical Technician Certificate, Laramie Community College, Laramie, WY
CPR Certification, American Red Cross *(current)*
BLS Certification, American Red Cross *(current)*

PRISON TRAINING FORMAT

(Best used to highlight general and/ or specialized training received in prison; can be used with either a chronological or a functional resume format)

EDUCATION

Maryland Department of Education　Baltimore, Maryland
GED Program Graduate, 2005
Maryland Department of Education　Jessup, Maryland
Career Exploration Certificate, 2004

If you don't like the words "Training and Education" for this section on your resume, there are many other titles that you can select from. Take your pick from the list that follows:

Educational Credentials　　Technical Training　　Professional Training
Educational Achievements　Continuing Education　Academic Experience

Other Resume Sections

Depending on your specific situation, your skills, background, experience, and qualifications, there may be other sections that you'll want to include on your resume. You should only include this type of information if it is relevant to you, your experience, and your current career goals.

TECHNOLOGY SKILLS AND QUALIFICATIONS

Applications:	Microsoft Office Suite; MS Project
Databases:	MS Access
Platforms:	Windows 2000/NT/95/98/ME/XP
Multimedia:	Media Player; Quick Time; Real Player
Networks:	Cisco VPN Altiga, Cisco Wireless Aironet; Net Store
Email:	Lotus Notes; Eudora; Netscape Mail

VOLUNTEER EXPERIENCE

Volunteer Caregiver, Piedmont Nursing Home (3 years)
Provided basic care and hygiene for elderly residents.

Childcare Provider, Riverwoods Community (1 year)
Provided free childcare to working mothers in an inner-city neighborhood.

Candy Striper, Metropolitan Hospital Center (2 years)
Assisted nursing staff with patient care and transportation.

HONORS AND AWARDS

- Class Achievement Award, State of Florida, 2005
- Athletic Achievement Award, State of Florida, 2004
- Perfect Attendance Award, Global Corporation, 2003
- Honors Graduate, St. Paul High School, 1997
- All-Conference Award (Basketball), St. Paul High School, 1997

MEMBERSHIPS

- Member, Automotive Engineering Society, 1990 to Present
- Member, Electrical Engineering Society, 1992 to Present
- Treasurer, Smithwood Town Association, 2001-2002
- Secretary, Smithwood Town Association, 2000-2001

Personal Information

There are several important issues you need to consider when determining whether or not to include a Personal Information section on your resume. Here are our recommendations:

Don'ts

- **DO NOT** include the fact that you were in prison on your resume. That is a discussion best managed one-on-one during a personal job interview.
- **DO NOT** include personal information such as birth date, marital status, health, number of children, and the like.
- **DO NOT** include the fact that you enjoy sports, camping, reading, and basketball. None of that is relevant to your job search, particularly early on when you are simply trying to get your foot in the door for an interview.

Do's

- **DO** include personal information if it is required by the employer.
- **DO** include personal information if important to clarify your citizenship or residency status.

- **DO** include personal information that is unique. We've worked with job seekers who were past Olympians, raced as competitive triathletes, trekked through regions worldwide, and much more. This is great information to include on your resume because it's unique and employers will remember you. Use whatever you have to get in the door!

If, after reading the above information, you have decided that including personal information is appropriate for your situation, consider the following format:

PERSONAL INFORMATION:
U.S. Citizen since 1994 (native of Mexico)
Fluent in English and Spanish
Competitive Soccer Player

The Resume Writing Process

Everything in life has a process, and resume writing is no different. If you use the following structured outline, you will find that the task of writing and producing your resume is faster, more efficient, and much easier.

1. **Open a file in your PC** and select a typestyle that (1) you like and (2) is easy to read. Type your name, address, email address, and phone numbers (home and cell).

2. **Type in all the major headings** you will be using (Career Objective, Skills Summary, Education, Work Experience).

3. **Fill in the basic information** for all of the sections that you are using except Work Experience. Don't worry about formatting, exact wording, or anything else. Just get the correct information into each of the sections.

4. **Carefully review all of the information** in each section and edit as necessary to improve the wording and visual presentation. Be sure to double-check that you have not omitted any important information.

5. **Write your job descriptions for chronological resumes – from past to present.** Start with the very first position you ever held and work forward. The older jobs are quick and easy to write. They're short and to the point, and should include only highlights of your most significant responsibilities and achievements, since they were so long ago. Then, as you work forward, each position requires a bit more information and a bit more thought to be sure that you've included all of the important information. Before you know it, you will be writing your current (or most recent) job description. This section will generally take the longest to write, but once it is finished, your resume will be 90% complete. If you're using a functional resume, this section should be quick and easy to complete.

6. **Write your Skills Summary.** This is the trickiest part of resume writing and can be the most difficult. At this point, you may want to re-read the preceding section in this chapter on writing skills summaries. Be sure to highlight your most notable skills, qualifications, and achievements as they relate to your current objectives and create a section that prominently communicates, "This is who I am and this is the value I bring to your company."

7. **Add boldface, italics, underlining, and other type enhancements** to draw visual attention to important information. This should include your name at the top of the resume, major headings, job titles, and any significant skills or achievements. You may also insert lines and/or boxes to offset key information, but be careful. Overuse of type enhancements will crowd your resume and make it appear "overdone." If you highlight too much, the resume appears cluttered and nothing stands out, clearly defeating your purpose.

8. **Carefully review the visual presentation.** How does your resume look? If your resume is two pages, does it break well between pages? Is it easy to read? Does it look professional? Even more important, does it convey the "right" message about "who" you are? At this point, you may need to adjust your spacing, change to a different typestyle, or make other minor adjustments to improve the visual appearance of your resume.

9. **Proofread your resume a minimum of three times.** Then, have one or two other people proofread it. It must be perfect, for nothing less is acceptable. Remember, people are meeting a piece of paper and not you. Make your first impression a powerful one.

Getting Started

The hardest part of any project is getting started, and writing your resume is no different. To help you overcome writer's block and other barriers that might be slowing you down, and to ensure that you get off to a strong start, look closely at the samples throughout this book to get ideas for resume format, design, wording, and presentation. Then, refer to Appendices A, B, and C, where you'll find three great resources to help you develop and write the content of your resume:

Appendix A – Resume Writing Worksheets
Appendix B – Action Verbs
Appendix C – Personality Descriptors

With all these great resources in hand, you have the tools that you need to write and design a powerful resume that is guaranteed to open doors, get interviews, and help you land a great job!

Chronological Resume Samples

FOLLOWING ARE 18 SAMPLE chronological resumes that you can use to get ideas for how to write and design your own winning resume. These are actual resumes of ex-offenders from prisons throughout the United States, although the names, addresses, phone numbers, company names, and other information have been changed to protect each person's privacy.

Examples as Learning Tools

Our examples are learning tools for understanding how each section of a chronological resume should be designed and written for job seekers with different goals, interests, skills, experiences, and accomplishments. Remember, most employers are busy people who may spend no more than 30 seconds reviewing a single resume! A resume must both catch and hold the reader's attention if it is to become a serious effort at getting a job interview.

Pay particular attention to both the form and content of each resume. What exactly grabs and holds the attention of the reader in each case? **Form** includes such elements as format, design, headings, typestyles, highlighting, and use of white space. Form deals with many of the cosmetic elements that make a resume attractive or pleasing to the eye – gives it "curb appeal" – even before the reader has a chance to read each section of the resume.

On the other hand, **content** deals with messages being communicated through specific words and phrases. A resume should clearly communicate, through the choice of words and phrases, what a candidate has done, can do, and will do in the future. Employers look for cues, both positive and negative, of future performance in their organization. They look for possible red flags that could eliminate you from further consideration. Those red flags come in many different forms – misspelled words, poor grammar, major time gap, lack of relevant education and experience, and things you should never put on your resume, such as salary information, references, and personal information.

Using Our Examples Wisely

As you examine our examples, keep in mind how you plan to write each section of **your** resume. While you should never copy the content of someone else's resume, you can copy the form and creatively "borrow" content from our examples by adopting many of the principles incorporated in our resumes. You can do this by:

- Copying formats and designs that you like.
- Using similar headings and typestyles.
- Selecting words in job descriptions that match what you did at a similar job.
- Creating similar wording in skills summaries that coincide with your own skills.
- Getting ideas for how to highlight your training, degrees, certifications, and licenses.
- Developing "short stories" about each of your skills and experiences that you can communicate verbally when networking and interviewing for a job.

In the end, your resume should be based on sound writing principles and strategy, as well as be employer-oriented and reflect the real you. Learn from our examples, but write your own resume based on information about yourself.

Our Winning Cast of Characters

To understand why these resumes were written and designed the way that they were, read the following information about each one as you review it.

Resume:	**LaTonya Anderson**, page 76
Prison:	2004 to Present (early 2006 release)
Writer:	Elizabeth Crimi, Maryland Correctional Institution for Women
Objective:	Position as a Cashier
Strategy:	Clearly state objective, follow with short skills summary, and then list all employment experience to demonstrate (1) solid work history and (2) prior experience as a cashier. Dates excluded to draw attention away from the fact that this client is currently incarcerated and, as such, unemployed.

Resume:	**Barbara R. Brown**, page 77
Prison:	2003 to 2005
Writer:	Elizabeth Crimi, Maryland Correctional Institution for Women
Objective:	Any one of a number of different types of positions (clerical, medical assisting, and/or lab operations) within the medical field
Strategy:	Follow objective with a summary of her skills in each of her three areas of interest within the medical field, and then showcase her strong record of work experience. Dates included to show reasonably up-to-date employment and direct experience with current medical practices. Explanation for unemployment since 2003 to be discussed during interview.

Resume:	**Eddie Bell**, page 78
Prison:	2000 to 2003
Writer:	Gina Taylor, Gina Taylor & Associates
Objective:	Position as a Truck Driver
Strategy:	Headline format clearly identifies job objective and is followed by an excellent summary of relevant experience, licenses, and professional designations. Employment history follows, demonstrating long-time experience as a driver and highlighting current employment. Jobs held while in prison were directly related to current employment objectives and were summarized under Fort Leavenworth job.

Resume:	**George S. Gonsalves**, page 79
Prison:	2001 to 2003
Writer:	Lee Ann Grundish, Gravix Services, Etc.
Objective:	Position as a Survey Technician

Strategy: Headline format used to clearly identify job objective, followed by a brief, easy-to-read summary of relevant skills and qualifications. Work experience showcases 15+ years experience as a surveyor and includes his experience while incarcerated (Monroe County Department of Roads). Strong educational qualifications and current professional affiliation further strengthen resume presentation.

Resume: **Rita D. Smith**, page 80
Prison: 2003 to Present (Spring 2006 release)
Writer: Gina Taylor, Gina Taylor & Associates
Objective: Position as an Office Receptionist or Office Administrator
Strategy: Headline format clearly presents objective and highlights relevant skills required for such a position. Experience section focuses on her current enrollment in Microsoft-certified courses (while incarcerated) to expand her office technology skills in preparation for release.   Other experience included to demonstrate track record of successful employment.

Resume: **Karen Marlowe**, page 81
Prison: 2000 to 2005
Writer: Louise Garver, Career Directions, LLC
Objective: Position as a Payroll Support Professional
Strategy: Excellent professional summary with a clear and concise presentation of her objective and her qualifications in first section. Focus of resume is on her employment experience (over 2/3 of the page), including her current position with Kelly Services, which she began immediately after her release from prison in the spring of 2005. Kelly Services job shows "present" with dates intentionally omitted so that no gap appears between 2000 and 2005, leaving an employer to believe that she's been with Kelly since 2002 when she left Warner Packaging.

Resume: **Jeanne Stanley**, page 82
Prison: 2004 to Present (December 2005 release)
Writer: Constance Parker, Maryland Correctional Institution for Women
Objective: Position as an Executive Chef
Strategy: Clear objective summarizing years of experience followed by

detailed employment experience section that demonstrates wide range of skills and qualifications that qualify her for her targeted position. Note the "current" Executive Chef position with Rightman Enterprises, which is her own company that she's operated on and off since 1994 (not currently active while incarcerated, but still owns the company).

Resume:	**Lamont Jabbar**, page 83
Prison:	1998 to 2002
Writer:	Melanie Noonan, Peripheral Pro, LLC
Objective:	Position as a Teacher or Counselor
Strategy:	Excellent skills and qualifications presented in detailed summary section, which is immediately followed by strong educational credentials. Field experience presented in detail to highlight overall scope of responsibility in both positions while drawing special attention to relevant projects, programs, and activities. No mention of incarceration, which occurred prior to start of his current career field.

Resume:	**Bonnie M. DeViers**, page 84
Prison:	1994 to 1998
Writer:	Lee Anne Grundish, Grafix Services, Etc.
Objective:	Position as a Librarian
Strategy:	Resume showcases 11 years of progressively responsible work experience – from a Resource Center Aide (while incarcerated) to a Library Assistant to a Librarian. Qualifications supported by strong educational credentials – a Bachelor of Arts degree earned while incarcerated and a more recent Master of Library Science degree. Clearly presents an individual who has changed her life and is already a productive member of the workforce.

Resume:	**John L. Trenton**, page 85
Prison:	2004 to 2005
Writer:	Wendy Enelow, Enelow Enterprises, Inc.
Objective:	Position as a Sales Representative
Strategy:	One-year prison term totally hidden in this resume, which showcases his work experience and strong qualifications in sales, revenue growth, and cost reduction. Detailed summary highlights

all relevant sales and client skills in a easy-to-read and quick-to-review format. Unemployment since 2004 left for discussion during interview.

Resume:	**Selena Warwick**, page 86
Prison:	2004 to 2005
Writer:	Michele Angello, Corbel Communications
Objective:	Position as a Property Manager
Strategy:	Began resume with thorough presentation of skills and experience, with greatest emphasis on her background in property maintenance to support her current career goals. Utilized standard chronological presentation of work history, using only years of employment to mask months of unemployment throughout her career. Focused job descriptions, as best as possible, on related property maintenance and management skills and not on her personal care responsibilities.

Resume:	**Daniel J. Davison**, page 87
Prison:	1990 to 2000
Writer:	Lee Anne Grundish, Grafix Services, Etc.
Objective:	Position as a Social Worker
Strategy:	Highlighted distinguishing professional credentials (MSW, CCDC) required for successful employment within the field of social work, a brief overview of core skills, and then short, but comprehensive job descriptions. Work experience clearly demonstrates his qualifications as a social worker and effectively masks his 10 years of imprisonment (summarized under Group Facilitator job with the State of Wisconsin).

Resume:	**Jeremy Campbell**, page 88
Prison:	1999 to 2005
Writer:	Janice Shepherd, Write On Career Keys
Objective:	Position as the Assistant Director for the Center for Troubled Youth
Strategy:	Unique presentation beginning with objective written specifically for the position for which he was applying. Followed with excellent presentation of skills and competencies in two sections (Profile and Qualifications). Work experience highlighted three dis-

tinct types of positions and focused on positive skills acquired from each. Position held while incarcerated (Kitchen Supervisor at the Men's Correctional Facility) presented in such a way that an employer would be inclined to interpret that as a "paid job" and not as a "prison job."

Resume:	**Kevin Johnson**, page 89
Prison:	1999 to 2003
Writer:	Jane Roqueplot, Janeco's Sensible Solutions
Objective:	Position in Social Services or Client Care
Strategy:	Headline format and strong summary section clearly position him as a well-qualified Social Services and Client Care Professional. Excellent job descriptions focus on skills, responsibilities, and diversity of client populations served, while downplaying dates of employment to draw attention away from four-year period of unemployment while incarcerated. List of continuing professional education and certificates further substantiates client's skills and competencies.

Resume:	**Donald R. Peterson**, page 90
Prison:	1995 to Present (late 2005 release)
Writer:	Melanie Noonan, Peripheral Pro, LLC
Objective:	Position as a Prison Minister
Strategy:	Ten-year prison record masked effectively by focusing on his newfound passion for the prison ministry. Unique format begins with a Bible quote and then a personal perspective. Work experience follows with emphasis on his experience at the Cabrini Treatment Center. Job description effectively highlights his contributions without disclosing his actual imprisonment.

Resume:	**Stephen J. Marshall**, pages 91-92
Prison:	2004 to Present (early 2006 release)
Writer:	Michael Davis, The Michaels Group
Objective:	Position as an IT Design Engineer or Project Manager
Strategy:	Excellent example of a well-written and well-designed resume for a technology industry professional. Begins with a headline and summary that clearly identify his strengths and qualifications, and is followed by thorough job descriptions that highlight his

skills, technical competencies, project highlights, and achievements. Education and technical credentials close the resume on a very positive note. Current incarceration not reflected on resume; to be discussed during interview.

Resume:	**Mark Frankfore**, page 93
Prison:	2000 to 2002
Writer:	Veda Jeffries, Stanford University
Objective:	Undecided; open to numerous opportunities
Strategy:	Began resume with broad-based summary of a diversity of skills that would coincide with any one of a number of different opportunities he might pursue. Followed with detailed overview of work experience; most notably, his career as an entrepreneur (1994 to present). This part-time position he'd engaged in for the past 10+ years covered the gap of employment left by his incarceration. Included a detailed education section to show his commitment to advancing his skills and knowledge. Additional information section used to round out his experience and showcase some of his personal characteristics.

Resume:	**Ronald Graham**, page 94
Prison:	1998 to 1999
Writer:	Jane Roqueplot, JaneCo's Sensible Solutions
Objective:	Undecided; open to various professional and semi-professional opportunities
Strategy:	Broad-based skills presented in Qualifications Summary to position him for a diversity of opportunities, followed by "traditional" chronological presentation of work experience and key responsibilities. Included position with the Cookie Factory (contracted with local prison for assembly and shipping) while he was incarcerated.

Resume:	**Mary Ling**, pages 95-96
Prison:	2002 to Present (late 2005 release)
Writer:	Linda Martel, Career Consultant/Coach
Objective:	Position in the Financial Products and/or Services industry.
Strategy:	Outstanding resume presentation for a financial industry professional. Begins with excellent overview of career in Profile sec-

tion and follows with comprehensive job descriptions that focus on results and accomplishments. Finishes with excellent presentation of educational qualifications and computer skills. Period of unemployment since incarcerated in 2002 to be discussed during interview.

LaTONYA ANDERSON

908 Lexington Street
Baltimore, Maryland 21205
410-652-3726

OBJECTIVE: To obtain a position as a Cashier.

SKILLS: Meets Deadlines
Accepts Responsibilities
Attends to Customers with Care

WORK EXPERIENCE:

Plummer Agency, Baltimore, Maryland
Assembly Line Worker
Presorted and packaged numerous items.

McDonald's, Baltimore, Maryland
Cashier/Prep Cook

Popeye's, Baltimore, Maryland
Cashier/Prep Cook

Manpower Temporary Agency, Columbia, Maryland
Assembly Line Worker
Presorted and packaged merchandise for two companies.

Domino's Pizza, Baltimore, Maryland
Cashier/Prep Cook

EDUCATION:

Maryland State Department of Education, Baltimore, Maryland
Career Exploration Certificate (105 Hours)

St. Mary's High School, Dundalk, Maryland
General Studies Program

BARBARA R. BROWN

12 Goodview Avenue
Westminster, MD 21157

Home 310-772-3827
brownfam@aol.com

OBJECTIVE: To obtain a challenging position in which I can utilize my skills and experience in the Medical field.

SKILLS: **Over 8 years of experience in the Medical field:**

- Positive attitude, organized, reliable, and detail-oriented.

- **Clerical skills** include medical terminology, scheduling surgery and appointments, medical billing, ICD-9 coding, and Microsoft Word.

- **Medical assisting skills** include back office, minor office surgeries and procedures, EKG testing, venipuncture, injections, CPR, first aid, and stress testing.

- **Lab experience** includes preparing blood and urine samples for lab transport and preparing biopsies for pathology departments.

EXPERIENCE: Marcus R. Wrightsman, M.D., Towson, Maryland
Certified Medical Assistant
2001 to 2003

The Towson Pediatric Group, Towson, Maryland
Certified Medical Assistant
1998 to 2001

St. Agnes Hospital, Baltimore, Maryland
Phlebotomist / Certified Medical Assistant
1997 to 1998

Lewis Medical Associates, Baltimore, Maryland
Certified Medical Assistant
1996 to 1997

EDUCATION: Medix School, Towson, Maryland
Medical Assistant Certificate – 1996

Howard County Vocational Technical Center, Columbia, Maryland
Practical Nursing Diploma – 1989

Dunbar High School, Dunbar, Maryland
High School Diploma – 1982

EDDIE BELL

1807 New Jersey • Kansas City, Kansas 66102
Phone: 913-488-6827 • Email: ebell298@sprintpcs.com

TRUCK DRIVER

- Driving experience operating flatbeds and dump trucks with a ***perfect*** driving record.
- Proficient in the operation of uniloaders, forklifts, front-end loaders, power sweepers, chain saws, and hydraulic grinders.

License/Professional Designation

Class A & Class B Commercial Driver's License
Endorsements: PTX
Passenger - Double/Triple Trailers
Combination of Tank Vehicle and Hazardous Materials

EMPLOYMENT HISTORY

FLEMING-BABCOCK, INC., Riverside, MO   April 2004 - Present
DRIVER
Haul asphalt, rock, concrete, and dirt. Maintain fuel logs and records of daily revenue.

FORT LEAVENWORTH, Fort Leavenworth, KS   2000 - 2003
DRIVER & CREW CHIEF - Roads & Grounds
Drove equipment for tree trimming and removal. Loaded and hauled dirt, sand, concrete slabs, and rock.
BANQUET COORDINATOR
EDUCATIONAL CLERK

FERGUSON PLUMBING SUPPLY, Shawnee, KS   1998 - 1999
DRIVER

TEXTILE SUPPLY, Merriam, KS   1997 - 1998
DRIVER

EDUCATIONAL BACKGROUND

Fort Scott Community College   Fort Scott, KS
TRUCK DRIVING I & II

❖ Defensive Driving	❖ Driving Task	❖ Range Driving
❖ Road Skills	❖ Backing	❖ Safe Driving Practices
❖ Driver's Daily Logs	❖ Equipment Familiarization	❖ Preventive Maintenance

Continued Professional Development:
Certificate: Automotive Prevention and Maintenance, 1997
Certificate: Electrical Training, 2002

GEORGE S. GONSALVES

812 Blackmaine Drive
Temperance, Michigan 48182
(734) 992-7246

CERTIFIED SURVEY TECHNICIAN

SURVEYING INSTRUMENTS:
* Electronic Total Station Equipment (Wild T-1000; Sokkia Set 5A)
* Level (to Obtain Elevations) * Engineers' Steel Tapes * Plumb Bobs

TECHNICAL SKILLS:
* CAD (Computer Aided Design) * Blueprint Reading/Interpretation

HIGH RATE OF PRECISION:
* Average Error of Closure 1:45,000

WORK EXPERIENCE

INSTRUMENT PERSON, *David E. Johnson and Associates, Inc.*, Dove Lake, Michigan   2003–Present
- **Surveying:** on-site operation of total station instrumentation for mortgage surveys, boundary delineation, and construction projects (setting grades and fabricating cut sheets for sewers).

CREW LEADER, *Monroe County Department of Roads*, Monroe County, Michigan   2001–2002
- **Transportation Engineering:** supervised 8-member team in surveys for roadway design and construction.
- **Emergency Road Team:** repairs and re-grading.

SURVEY TECHNICIAN, *Mason, Prater and Smith*, Edgerton, Ohio   1990–2000
- **Surveying:** coordinated 3 crews at multiple sites in construction staking of road projects.

EDUCATION

SURVEY TECHICIAN CERTIFICATION TRAINING, *Michigan Society of Professional Surveyors*   1992
ASSOCIATE OF APPLIED SCIENCE DEGREE, SURVEYING, *Marvin College*, Marvin, Michigan   1990

PROFESSIONAL ASSOCIATION

Affiliate Member, Michigan Society of Professional Surveyors   1990-Present

RITA D. SMITH

212 Grayson Lane • Topeka, Kansas 67362
909.727.6262

OFFICE RECEPTIONIST or OFFICE ADMINISTRATOR

Well-organized and versed in many areas of sales, customer service, and telephone communication. Computer proficient in Word, Excel, Access, and PowerPoint; Internet experience. Possess excellent telephone and communication skills.

- ❖ Excels under pressure
- ❖ Self-disciplined
- ❖ Quick learner
- ❖ Motivated
- ❖ Problem solver
- ❖ Great people skills

PROFESSIONAL EXPERIENCE

T.C.F., TOPEKA, KANSAS   2005- PRESENT
MICROSOFT CERTIFIED COURSES

WAL-MART, STEVENSON RANCH, CALIFORNIA   2001-2003
CUSTOMER SERVICE REPRESENTATIVE
- Coordinated customer service and returns.
- Answered phones.

STONE CREEK APARTMENTS, LANCASTER, CALIFORNIA   1998-2001
LEASING AGENT
- Drew-up rental agreements, conducted walk-throughs, and performed credit checks.
- Deposited collections.
- Answered phones, filed, and performed data entry.

PRIVATE HEALTH CARE, SANTA CLARITA, CALIFORNIA   1994-1998
CERTIFIED NURSE ASSISTANT
- In-home care of patient with renal failure and diabetes.
- Transported patient to doctor and physical therapy appointments.

CIVIC/COMMUNITY INVOLVEMENT

SANTA CLARITA COMMUNITY CENTER
P.T.A. - PLACERITA JR. HIGH AND WILEY COUNTY ELEMENTARY

-REFERENCES AVAILABLE UPON REQUEST-

KAREN MARLOWE

8667 Sorren Avenue • Granby, CT 06087 • (860) 599–5008

PAYROLL SUPPORT PROFESSIONAL

Experienced in providing office/payroll support, data entry, and customer service. Computer skills include MS Word, Excel, and PowerPoint. Demonstrated ability to learn new skills quickly and effectively. Bilingual in English and Spanish. Able to work independently and as part of a team.

EMPLOYMENT

KELLY SERVICES
Hartford, CT

Office/Payroll Clerk (Present)

- Maintain up-to-date files and records, including entering changes in insurance coverage, job titles, and department transfers.
- Compile summaries of earnings, taxes, deductions, leave, disability, and nontaxable wages for report preparation.
- Calculate employee federal and state income and Social Security taxes and employer's Social Security, unemployment, and workers' compensation payments.
- Research and resolve payroll discrepancies in a timely manner.
- Enter customer billing information in an accurate and timely manner.

WARNER PACKAGING
Hartford, CT

Receptionist/Customer Service (1995 to 2000)

- Greeted visitors; answered busy multi-line telephone systems; screened and transferred calls while handling general inquiries.
- Addressed customer concerns, researching and resolving problems to ensure service satisfaction.
- Communicated extensively with all internal departments and personnel.

FENMORE INC.
Hartford, CT

Office Support (1989 to 1995)

- Provided support to 3 departments: word processing documents, creating PowerPoint presentations, and maintaining confidential files/records.
- Scheduled and coordinated meetings and appointments.
- Ordered and maintained department supplies inventory.

EDUCATION

Manchester Community College, Manchester, CT
Accounting courses

JEANNE A. STANLEY
8076 Greenbrier Avenue, Apt. 201
Silver Spring, Maryland 20910
Home Phone: 301-909-7263
Email: chefstanley@netscape.com

OBJECTIVE: Executive Chef position utilizing my 20 years' experience and skills in culinary arts.

EXPERIENCE: Rightman Enterprises, Claytorville, Maryland
Executive Chef (Contract) – 1994 to Present

- Negotiated contracts with agents and representatives for catered events.

- Coordinate activities of kitchen personnel and supervise meal preparation.

- Create and present menus for a wide range of special events.

Goldman's Deli, Pikesville, Maryland
Deli Chef – 2000 to 2004

- Supervised, coordinated, and participated in activities of cooks and other kitchen personnel.

- Measured and mixed ingredients according to recipes, using a variety of kitchen utensils and equipment (e.g., blenders, mixers, grinders, slicers, tenderizers).

- Trained personnel in all aspects of food handling, temperature control, cross contamination, and proper storage of food and food products.

Jesse's Catering Connections, Baltimore, Maryland
Contract Caterer – 1995 to 2000

- Coordinated food service for hotels, restaurants, special events, social functions, and other establishments/clients.

- Consulted with food preparation and other personnel to plan menus and coordinate event set-up.

- Responded to written and telephone requests for future functions.

EDUCATION: The School of Culinary Arts, Charleston, South Carolina
Certified Chef – 1995
Master Baker – 1993

REFERENCES: Available Upon Request

LAMONT JABBAR

2450 Holbrook Avenue, Chicago, IL 60607
(312) 555-5555

SUMMARY

Teacher and counselor of youth and adults, dedicated to overcoming their obstacles to learning and instilling in them the skills necessary to be productive members of society. Outstanding ability to relate to student needs and increase their motivation to succeed. Major strength in organizing resources and participants for special programs.

Populations served: High school dropouts or adult returnees of all ages; parolees; the homeless, unskilled, unemployed, or mentally impaired; and recovering alcoholics or substance abusers.

Areas of effectiveness:
- High school diploma/GED preparation
- High school proficiency testing/academic assessment
- Basic skills and adult life skills instruction

EDUCATION
- Career exploration/aptitude testing
- Crisis intervention

University of Chicago – **B.A., Social Science, *cum laude*, 2004**

FIELD
EXPERIENCE

M.A. Candidate

Illinois Certifications: Basic Skills Instructor; Teacher, K-8
Certificates in Trauma Counseling and Alcohol/Substance Abuse Counseling expected 2006

CHICAGO BOARD OF EDUCATION   2004–20 05
ADULT LEARNING CENTER AT SOUTHSIDE HIGH SCHOOL
Internship as GED Instructor and Life Skills Educator
- Taught adult groups totaling over 250 enrollees ranging in age from 16 to 47, helping them to acquire their high school diploma, develop their job search skills, or prepare them for continuing education.
- Assessed individual academic needs, recommending courses related to their career direction and educational level.
- Handled administrative functions, which included coordinating activity schedules for a 20-member teaching staff and enforcing discipline.
  – Develop ed program enhancement, "Success Seminar," and served as its instructor. Motivated participants' career interests by supplementing lectures with guest speakers from the business community.
  – Created an atmosphere conducive to learning, which has produced a 95% student retention rate through graduation.

COMMUNITY-BASED PROJECTS   2002–Pres ent
- Participated in a tutorial project designed to upgrade the math and reading skills of 40 students who scored below normal on standardized achievement tests.
- Trained high school students to tutor 4th graders in an educational enrichment program that was mutually rewarding to both groups.
- Assisted in the implementation of a state-funded program to select and train eligible candidates for entry-level service positions in office, industrial, and hospital settings.

Bonnie M. DeViers

894 Tulip Lane
Tiffin, Ohio 44883

(419) 624-2644
BD@grafixservices.com

LIBRARIAN: CAREER SUMMARY

A Master's-level professional with more than ten years' progressive experience in library science in a variety of areas: public library services, academics, museum resources, preservation, and storage of historical archives, and a busy, urban medical center library.

EXPERIENCE

LIBRARIAN, *City of Tiffin Library*, Tiffin, Ohio   2002 – Present
- **Library Operations:** Collaborate with professional and volunteer staff to implement and monitor industry and institutional policies, methods, programs, and circulation of 200,000 items annually.
- **Patron Services:** Build and maintain positive rapport with diverse personalities of all ages and backgrounds. Conduct searches; access and generate a broad range of multimedia reference sources and archival/stack collections; provide information and recommendations.

LIBRARY ASSISTANT, *Midwest Health System*, Columbus, Ohio   1999 – 2002
- **Medical Library Administration** for fast-paced healthcare complex serving 285 physicians. Assisted doctors and medical students in conducting research studies and compiling data for reports.
- **Circulation:** Checked materials in and out; processed requests, reserves, and renewals; returned items to shelving; conducted inspections; routed materials for mending, rebinding, or discarding.

RESOURCE CENTER AIDE, *State of Ohio*, Marion, Ohio   1994 – 1998
- **Library Support:** Assisted system users in locating reading and resource materials from card catalog featuring 10,000 items (books, periodicals, and video- and sound-recordings).

EDUCATION

MASTER OF LIBRARY SCIENCE, *Wittenberg University*, Springfield, Ohio   2002
- **American Library Association (ALA) Accredited Program**

BACHELOR OF ARTS, HISTORY, *The Ohio State University*, Columbus, Ohio   1997

ASSOCIATIONS

OHIO LIBRARY COUNCIL: Northwest Conference Attendee   2002 – Present
GREAT LAKES HISTORICAL SOCIETY: Secretary/Recorder   2002 – Present

TECHNOLOGY / COMPUTER SKILLS

* Microsoft Word; Excel; PowerPoint; Access; Outlook; Publisher * Internet Research / Communication
* SIRSI Unicorn   * DRA Classic (Data Research Associates)   * Bar Code Scanning Equipment

JOHN L. TRENTON

1702 Elm Road — San Diego, CA 99078

616-976-5471 — jltrent@aol.com

SALES REPRESENTATIVE

Building Sales Revenues & Expanding Sales Channels

Self-confident and motivated with good track record in sales and construction with start-up companies. Communicate clearly and effectively with people of diverse backgrounds. Use tact and patience when dealing with difficult customers. Goal oriented and persuasive. Areas of expertise:

- Budgeting
- Strategic Planning
- Problem Solving

- Relationship Selling
- Account Development
- Negotiation

- Customer Service
- Training
- Team Building

RELATED SALES EXPERIENCE

Sales Rep

David's Home Builders & Contractors, San Diego, CA, 1999–2004
Start-up to high-growth residential and commercial construction company

Prospected new accounts utilizing a variety of effective sales techniques including cold calling, direct mail, and telephone campaigns. Emphasized service, quality, and price. Handled bids, accurately estimating materials and labor costs for remodeling and new construction. Located hard-to-find materials and supplies; arranged for on-time delivery. Kept records of jobs to determine profitability. Supervised construction crews of up to 65 people; hands-on building experience.

- Grew business from 7 employees to 65.
- Drove revenues from zero to more than $4,000,000.

Manager

Palmer Custom Golf Clubs, San Dimon, CA, 1990–1998

Assessed golfers' level of expertise, utilizing knowledge of the sport, to design and build custom golf clubs. Promoted business through print advertising, networking, and customer service. Built and maintained client base and customer loyalty through quality product and service, resulting in high number of referrals.

- Slashed advertising budget 50% due to high-referral business and repeat clientele.

EDUCATION

San Diego High School, San Diego, CA: Diploma

Computer Experience: Windows, Microsoft Office, construction-specific software, and the Internet.

SELENA WARWICK

4255 Washington Street ♦ Denver, CO 80211 ♦ 303-657-8922
selena_warwick@hotmail.com

KEY QUALIFICATIONS

Dedicated, loyal employee with diverse career background. Proven ability to complete assigned projects on time while unsupervised or as an effective team member. Demonstrated ability to utilize available resources and follow through to completion. Possess strong work ethic with 100% dedication to assigned tasks. Work well with wide range of people. Capable of learning new skills rapidly.

- **PROPERTY MAINTENANCE** – Proven skills with troubleshooting and resolving problems. Expert in repairing and maintaining all household appliances, paint, windows, and landscaping. Strong ability to use hand tools and lay carpet.

- **HOSPITALITY** – Extensive experience in home health care, in addition to work background in restaurants and hotels, including practical experience as server, laundry worker, and housekeeper.

- **CLIENT RELATIONSHIPS** – Accomplished communicator with demonstrated ability to build trust and solidify relationships due to continued interest in and dedication to clients. Proven ability to influence and persuade.

WORK HISTORY

AFFORDABLE CARE, MINNEAPOLIS, MN   2004
Personal Care Provider
Provided live-in comprehensive care to quadriplegic client. Provided medical assistance, administered prescriptions, and performed physical therapy. Prepared all meals. Performed overall cleaning, including laundry. Oversaw proper maintenance of property including deep cleaning, window washing, and organization. Completed home repairs, including extensive painting, carpet laying, snow removal, weatherization, and landscaping. Entrusted with paying utility bills.

TRAFFIC STAFF SUPPORT, LAKEWOOD, CO   2001 – 2003
Flagger
Directed and safely controlled traffic through road construction sites on interstates, state highways, and city streets. Performed work responsibilities in all types of weather and hazardous areas/conditions.

WALLACE HOUSE, BROOMFIELD, CO   2000 – 2001
Laundry Tech/Housekeeper
Completed laundry and housekeeping in lockdown facility for troubled juveniles.

REUBEN ALLEN, THORNTON, CO   1997 – 2004
Personal Care Provider
Provided home care service, including all cleaning, laundry, and cooking. Accountable for painting, wallpaper hanging, general repairs, and gardening. Cared for patient at home after bypass heart surgery, including changing bandages and administering medications. Conducted physical therapy.
- Gained extensive experience with wood refinishing, plumbing repairs, deck construction, air conditioning repair, furnace lighting, water heater replacement, and landscape pruning.
- Earned trust and gratitude from client for excellent care. Built and maintained close relationship.

EVERGREEN CARE HOME, LAKEWOOD, CO   1996 – 1997
Certified Nurse's Aide
Assisted 57 Alzheimer patients with daily routine within locked facility. Performed feeding, bathing, and changing. Attained raises for dependable, solid performance of job duties.

EDUCATION & TRAINING

COLORADO STATE BOARD OF NURSING, Nurse's Aide Certificate
COLORADO DEPARTMENT OF TRANSPORTATION, Traffic Control Certificate
NORTHEASTERN COLLEGE, LIMON, CO, Secretarial Certificate

DANIEL J. DAVISON, MSW

2828 North Darewood Drive
Devonshire, Ohio 43623-2828
(419) 899-2387 (Phone/Fax)
DDAV223@grafixservices.com

CREDENTIALS

- Master of Social Work (MSW)
- Certificate of Specialization, Geriatrics
- Certified Chemical Dependency Counselor (CCDC)
- CPR Certification (Cardiopulmonary Resuscitation)

PROFESSIONAL SKILLS AND EXPERIENCE

- Mental Health Services
- Individual and Group Therapy
- Counseling
- Case Management
- Research Support
- Manuscript Assistance

EMPLOYMENT

RESEARCH ASSISTANT, *Dr. Henry Clark,* Devonshire, Ohio   2001 – Present
- **Project Support Clerk** for psychological studies; compile data; conduct qualitative and statistical analysis; compile reference sources and bibliographical citations according to American Psychological Association (APA) format; edit and transcribe texts.
- **Achievements:** Prepared 4 manuscripts accepted for publication in high-profile trade publications.

GROUP FACILITATOR, *State of Wisconsin,* Madison, Wisconsin   1990 – 2000
- **Discussion-Group Leader** on a variety of issues: anger and stress management, substance abuse/ chemical dependency, goal-setting, and daily living skills.
- **Achievement:** Increased participation in groups from 6 to 40 members.

LICENSED SOCIAL WORKER, *Wisconsin Youth Treatment Center,* Eau Claire, Wisconsin   1984 – 1990
- **Case Manager** for up to 15 youth, ages 5 to 18; individual counseling and group therapy on family issues, behavioral and emotional problems, suicidal thoughts/feelings, anger, anxiety, and abuse.

THERAPIST, *Vermeer School for Boys,* Bloomville, Indiana   1982 – 1984
- **Licensed Social Worker (LSW)** in residential treatment center for displaced children. Provided counseling services for 25 youth in preparation for home visits, reunification, and/or foster care.

EDUCATION

Master of Arts, Social Work, *Case Western Reserve University,* Cleveland, Ohio   1982
Bachelor of Arts, Sociology, *Columbia University,* New York, New York   1980

Jeremy Campbell

1234 New Town Lane
New Town, Washington 90880
(333-290-8080)

Objective: Assistant Director, Center for Troubled Youth

PROFILE

Possess understanding of business protocol, a pleasant attitude, and skills required to succeed in the position. Willing to learn, work hard, and apply a good work ethic.

Currently enrolled in business management class; consciously trying to make a positive impact by tutoring young people. Ability and desire to effectively communicate to kids first-hand why they want to change their lives now, before they waste their youth.

QUALIFICATIONS

- Excellent analytical and financial management skills.
- History of developing and maintaining loyal repeat customers.
- Excellent memory for names and faces.
- Proven strength in marketing without advertising.
- Skilled in recognizing and creating business opportunities.
- Demonstrated ability to successfully build upon limited resources.
- Speak fluent Spanish.

EXPERIENCE

Men's Correctional Facility, WA, 1999–2005
Kitchen Supervisor

- Directed activities and performance of 23 men in the preparation, service, and clean-up of meals for inmates.
- Applied strong leadership, conflict-resolution, and mediation skills. Monitored and kept records of kitchen inventory. Commended for consistent excellent management and job performance.

Self-Employed, throughout Washington State, 1995–1999
Pharmaceutical Sales

- Built and maintained loyal customer base.
- Created extensive contacts network.
- Managed cash flow.
- Kept accurate bookkeeping records.
- Polished communication and mediation skills.

Construction Laborer, part-time and seasonal work, various employers, 1987–1995

- Developed finish carpentry skills and learned to operate heavy equipment such as bulldozer, dump truck, and cement mixer. Worked with crews comprised of diverse backgrounds and personalities.

PROFESSIONAL DEVELOPMENT / EDUCATION

Business Management, Community College, WA, currently attending
Tutor/Advisor, Youth Group, Community Church
Graduate, New Town High School, WA

Kevin Johnson   412-555-0631

480 Butterfly Lane • Shippensburg, Pennsylvania 17257

SOCIAL SERVICES / CLIENT CARE
Community Resources • Child Welfare • Therapeutic Staff Support

✓ Service- and people-oriented. Effectively identify and resolve problems using available resources. Build confidence in others. Assured, diplomatic, and poised.

✓ Noteworthy communication skills. Interact positively with a wide range of people of various cultures and socio-economic backgrounds. Effective at giving verbal and non-verbal feedback to encourage people to be open, to trust, and to be receptive to suggestions. Skilled at negotiating conflicts.

✓ Prioritize workload and multi-task; flexible to changing priorities. Gather facts and supportive data to make decisions. Valued team player.

EMPLOYMENT HISTORY

Centers for Behavioral and Developmental Disabilities – Shippensburg, Pennsylvania   *2003– Present*
DIRECT CARE WORKER

- As member of 2-person team, provide complete Activity of Daily Living (ADL) assistance for three adult residents in a group home. Perform housekeeping tasks and cook meals. Ensure all residents receive proper meals, medication, hygiene, and basic care. Establish rapport and sense of trust with residents. Report all activities to supervisors.
- Keep files up-to-date (e.g., progress reports, house notes, and individual I.D. notes).
- Provide transportation to care programs, home visits, and recreational activities; supervise behavior of residents.

Highmark Counseling Services – Beaver, Pennsylvania   *2003*
St. John's Child Guidance Services – Beaver, Pennsylvania   *1997 – 1999*
THERAPEUTIC STAFF SUPPORT / WRAPAROUND WORKER

- Provided direct supervision of child to optimize educational, enrichment, and recreational activities. Reported to treatment intervention team for guidance in appropriate approach to behavior problem(s). Assisted with activities of daily living.
- Maintained up-to-date progress notes to guide treatment intervention. Recorded information regarding progression or regression in client's behaviors.

Jefferson Manor – Austintown, Ohio   *1989 – 1997*
CAREGIVER / COMMUNITY RESOURCES / ACTIVITIES COORDINATOR

- Directed activities and promoted community resources for 30+ residents living in three adult foster care/group homes within the community. Assisted with Activities of Daily Living (ADL).
- Transported residents to medical and community resources on consistent basis, facilitating improved therapeutic/medical results of treatment. Coordinated casework arrangements.

Youth Recreational Centers – Austintown, Ohio   *1984 – 1989*
PROGRAM WORKER

- Supervised recreational activities for children on site and on field trips. Provided guidance and served as role model for children.
- Conducted Adult Forum to establish and promote community-based civil humanities for both children and adults. Facilitated discussions on issues impacting relationships.

EDUCATION / CONTINUING EDUCATION / TRAINING

- Certificate, 2003, Safe Crisis Management, 12-hour course
- Certificate, 2001, Professional Ethics, Indiana State University
- Awareness Training, Indiana State University
- Certificate, 2001, Basic Understanding of Computers, Tri State Center
- Certificate, 1989, High Risk Children: Handle with Care, 3-day course,
     Family Recovery Center of Indiana County
- Certificate, Children and Adolescents, 1987, Parkview Counseling Center
- Certificate, Group Work for Human Relations and Development of Civil Harmonizing
- Coursework, Social Work Administration, 1987, Pennsylvania State University

B.A., Social Work, 1983, The Ohio State University
"A" Student in Field Work Placement Internship

Donald R. Peterson

1234 West 89th Street
New York, NY 10026
(212) 555-1212

DRP1234@worldnet.com

PRISON MINISTER

The Spirit of the Lord is upon me, because He hath anointed me to preach the gospel to the poor; He hath sent me to heal the broken-hearted, to preach deliverance to the captives, and recovering of sight to the blind, to set at liberty them that are bruised. [Luke 4:18]

Perspective

My eyes were opened to salvation through the kindness and understanding of a chaplain at Riker's Island State Prison. Just as his influence changed my life, I believe many people in the prison environment can be readily reached by my friend-making heart. God has given me this gift for meeting the spiritual and emotional needs of the incarcerated. Though they may be guarded or even brusquely defensive, their demeanor eventually softens as I win them over with my unconditional and persistent love.

Education

BETHANY DIVINITY COLLEGE, DALTON, AL (Distance Learning Program)
Certificate in Bible Studies, 2003
Bachelor's Degree in Christian Counseling, expected 2006

Pastoral Experience

CABRINI TRANSITIONAL CENTER, NEW YORK, NY   September 2004 to Present
Tutor/Mentor to 22 underachieving, teen male detainees
- Convinced many youth, including one who was suicidal, to abandon self-destructive behavior, as they came to see life through my presence and facilitating in a more positive light.
- Developed strategies to bring out dormant capabilities and personality aspects of almost all residents.
- Drew out some depressed residents to air their views and feelings.

Prior Work Experience

RICHFIELD PRODUCTS, BRONX, NY   1993–1995
Packing Machine Operator

ALL-BRITE CARPET CLEANING COMPANY, WESTCHESTER, NY   1989–1993
Rug Cleaner

GRAND CENTRAL COURIER SERVICE, NEW YORK, NY   1987–1988
Bicycle Messenger

Stephen J. Marshall

7717 Creekside Court, Clive, Iowa 50325

sjm6@copper.net   Mobile: (515) 789-5155   Residence: (515) 978-3839

IT DESIGN ENGINEER / PROJECT MANAGER

Software Development & Implementation / Testing / System Design & Integration
Quality Assurance / Leadership / Project Management / MCSE / Training Systems

Design, develop, and deliver innovative technology solutions to meet challenging business demands. Extensive qualifications in project management from feasibility studies, reviewing system design requirements, implementation, and testing to ongoing support. Excellent skills in cross-functional team-building and leadership. Keen problem-solving and decision-making skills.

PROFESSIONAL EXPERIENCE

CACI International, Inc., Des Moines, Iowa

Computer Scientist, 1996 - 2004

Provided day-to-day leadership and support to 4-person life-cycle development team for Contract Writing System for over 2,000 users.

- Analyzed, designed, and tested contract writing software using Visual Basic, Microsoft Office, and automated testing tools in the enterprise scale Windows XP/2000/NT environment. Produced superior product that exceeded customers' expectations.
- Coordinated with other departments to gather and publish user documentation, fix program bugs, test applications, develop help screens, and provide configuration management.

Business Analyst, 1995 - 1996

Analyzed computer software capabilities by testing all functions, conducted system training, and provided project support for a Deficiency Reporting System project.

- Analyzed computer software capabilities and conducted peer reviews for program technical standards and test plans. Performed statistical analysis on test results and quality assurance procedures for process engineering, business, and records management functions for all testing, training, and project support issues in a Software Engineering Institute (SEI) Level 3 environment.
- Led 6-person software testing team for Fortune 1000 IT company. Teamed with two software engineers to author testing procedures, supervised testing implementation, and documented test results. Ensured excellent product delivered to customer.

General Dynamics Corporation, Des Moines, Iowa

Systems Engineer, 1994 - 1995

Produced hard and electronic copy of Training Assessment for automated Management System.

- Evaluated process flow, organization, and planning problems within the Business Process Model. Led special projects, conducted functional analysis, reviewed system design requirements, and conducted feasibility studies for new product concepts to support implementation. Improved process efficiency by 10%.

Stephen J. Marshall   Page 2

PROFESSIONAL EXPERIENCE CONTINUED

North American Rockwell, Downey, California

> *Lead Systems Integration Engineer*, 1992 - 1994
> - Led Integrated Product Team (IPT). Coordinated with managers, engineers, logisticians, contractors, and customers managing Deficiency Reports. Tracked over 450 deficiencies simultaneously. Solved critical problems discovered during qualification and operational testing on $887 million aircraft program.
> - Researched and proposed using actual operational aircraft to integrate software and avionics during development phase. Avoided "fly-fix-fly" to repair aircraft deficiencies, which saved almost $1.5 million in man-hours, expensive flight-test time, fuel, and range time.

> *Training System Development Manager*, 1988 - 1992
> - Identified limitations in cockpit training procedures that saved over $500,000 by preventing purchase of obsolete equipment.
> - Coordinated implementation of off-the-shelf training management system. Fully met all requirements for scheduling and resource allocation. Saved over 2,000 man-hours and $8 million in development efforts.

EDUCATION and TRAINING

Master of Science (MS), *Computer Science*
GEORGIA TECH COLLEGE OF COMPUTING, Atlanta, Georgia, 1990

Bachelor of Science (BS), *Engineering Mechanics*
UCLA, Loa Angeles, California, 1988

CERTIFICATIONS

MCSE, *Microsoft Certified Systems Engineer*, 2000

MARK F. FRANKFORE

100 Morris Lane • Palo Alto, CA 90005 • 610-555-2983 • cell: 610-555-1873

SUMMARY OF QUALIFICATIONS:

- Excellent interpersonal communication, time management, and organizational skills.
- Assertive, self-motivated, goal-directed, and a team player.
- High degree of entrepreneurial and business logic.
- Effective performance in a multi-task work environment.
- Highly reliable, capable, and dependable. Thrive on change and respond in a positive manner to new responsibilities and tasks.

WORK EXPERIENCE:

Contract Driver, JOHNSON & JONES INDUSTRIES, Woodland, CA (10/02 – present)
Assigned territory in South Bay covering 10 accounts. Deliver auto parts to assigned auto dealers covering more than 300 miles. Work independently and plan and organize time assuring that parts are delivered in a timely manner. Work a flexible schedule that includes an occasional Saturday.

Entrepreneur, Palo Alto, CA (12/94 – present)
Purchase and sell American cars from auctions. Repair cars as needed to meet the Department of Motor Vehicle requirements. Advertise in the community and local newspapers and by word of mouth.

Accounts Payable Clerk, MILLS GENERAL HOSPITAL, Millbrae, CA (2/00 – 12/00)
Contracted by Adele Temporary Agency. Prepared and generated checks on a weekly basis; matched invoices to checks for review and approval. Coded and input recurring inventory and miscellaneous invoices daily for Headquarters and remote offices. Followed up on vendor questions and issues. Tracked orders and maintained purchase order log for marketing and miscellaneous purchase orders not generated by the system. Documented and revised policies and procedures on an on-going basis. Prepared expense accrual journal entries and recorded bank activity for checking account. Monthly, reconciled billable receivables, prepaid, and miscellaneous accounts. Managed special projects.

Administrative Assistant, ADELE CORPORATE OFFICE, Palo Alto, CA (12/99 – 2/00)
Worked under constant time constraints because Headquarters was relocating to New York and there was a time limit to complete tasks. Entered data as assigned by manager. Worked independently and was not closely supervised. Schedule was flexible and included occasional overtime.

COMPUTER SKILLS: Experienced with Macintosh. Software includes MS Word, Excel, PowerPoint, FileMaker Pro, and Lawson (accounting program).

EDUCATION:

San Jose State University, San Jose, CA
Humanities and Biology

San Jose City College, San Jose, CA
Sociology, Accounting, Computer Science/Business, English,
American History, and African American History in the United States

Laney College, Oakland, CA
English, History, Human Relations, Computer Science, Accounting, and Asian American History

College of San Mateo, San Mateo, CA
Math, English, History, and Business Law

Sequoia Institute, Fremont, CA
Specialized in auto mechanics. Coursework included repairing brakes, engines, and suspension

ADDITIONAL INFORMATION:

- Additional work experience includes other short-term assignments at Adele Temporary Agency, while attending college.
- Certified for CPR and First Aid
- Build remote control cars and airplanes. Collect video games. Enjoy restoring old cars.
- *Volunteer*, worked with children at Englewood Presbyterian Church & Community Center to plan activities for enrichment.

RONALD GRAHAM

P.O. Box 405 • Centerville, Pennsylvania 16404 • (814) 734-5234

QUALIFICATIONS SUMMARY

➢ Versatile, hardworking individual; driven to meet or exceed expectations. Demonstrate an exceptional work ethic.

➢ Entrusted with responsibility to handle cash; demonstrate accuracy in assigned tasks.

➢ Excellent organizational skills; detail oriented. Design delivery routes to capture time and fuel savings.

➢ Noted for mechanical aptitude; able to make repairs to keep machinery functioning. Skillfully use hand tools and machines.

➢ Represent employer in a professional manner and appearance. Make decisions and solve problems using facts and personal judgment.

➢ Effective interpersonal skills; work well as a team member with people at all levels of an organization and of various cultures. Equally capable working independently.

EMPLOYMENT

MORTGAGE BROKER
The Refinance Group, Inc. — Centerville, Pennsylvania — 2002 – Present

• Interview applicants applying for refinancing loans by phone and enter data into computer.

• Locate mortgage rates and find appropriate bank for customer. Submit mortgage loan application file for underwriting approval.

DELIVERY DRIVER / STOCK CLERK
KJU Catering Company — Connellsville, Pennsylvania — 2000 - 2002
Harris Auto Supply — Centerville, Pennsylvania — 1999
North Penn Snacks (Smart Corn Chips) — McDonald, Ohio — 1997 - 1998

• Commended for performing reliably and in a friendly manner. Stocked candy and soda vending machines. Maintained accurate inventory; placed orders to ensure adequate inventory on hand. Collected cash. Made minor repairs to vending machines as needed.

• Expediently delivered auto parts to businesses and private owners. Confirmed store deliveries and matched items to shipping document list. Ensured shelves remained stocked.

• Delivered chips and candy to schools throughout northeastern Ohio. Checked accuracy of orders. Complimented for efficient and timely deliveries.

BAKER'S ASSISTANT / SHIPPING / MAINTENANCE
The Cookie Factory — Centerville, Pennsylvania — 1998 - 1999

• Prepared dough to be used for dinner rolls and cookies. Operated dough mixers, cutters, tape machine, and bag sealer. Verified orders prior to shipping. Cleaned/sanitized entire work area daily per established procedures. Ensured customers received orders.

EDUCATION

Office Management Certificate, 1992, GPA 3.0
Charleston Job Corp Center – Charleston, West Virginia

Graduate, 1991, GPA 3.0
Boardwalk High School – Boardwalk, New Jersey

MARY LING

416-111-2121
maryling@rogers.com

532 Highland Crescent
Whitby, Ontario, L1A 9W2

PROFILE

- Energetic and results-focused team player with over 11 years' direct experience in financial products, sales, and services industries, accompanied with consistent, excellent results in all facets of business development.
- Versatile and flexible employee who adapts easily to change and thrives on new challenges and responsibilities.
- Possess strong communication and relationship-building skills ensuring clients experience a professional and value-added business relationship.
- Proven leader who relates well to diverse team members and takes pride in promoting teammates in personal and professional development.

PROFESSIONAL EXPERIENCE

CANADA TRADE BROKERS   **1998 – 2002**
Team Leader – National Business Development (2001 – 2002)

- 2002 Q1: Exceeded individual sales target by 250%, attaining 70% of the 2002 yearly asset target.
- Achieved 100% retention of a client list in excess of $60 million during a crucial high-level client retention campaign.
- Trained and oriented 20 non-client facing employees in a three-day intensive training session in areas of sales and services, internal computer systems, and administrative duties. Provided ongoing support to ensure that accuracy and service standards were met.
- Created a manual based on the eBusiness Client Relationship Management (CRM) system to enable consistent entry of prospect/client information by sales team.
- Provide leadership and guidance to the 14-member National Business Development team.
- Trained, coached, supervised, and motivated staff while maintaining good morale and fostering teamwork.
- Monitored team performance and, in conjunction with the Manager, completed performance reviews and set objectives for team members through quarterly performance appraisals.
- Revised procedures quarterly to increase administrative efficiencies, reduce potential liabilities, and ensure service standards were met.
- Assisted the Retail Trading Desk with timely execution of equity, mutual fund, and fixed-income orders, while maintaining Team Leader role.

National Business Development Specialist (1998 – 2001)

- Ranked #1 nationally in both new assets and account conversions accounting for over $23 million in new assets and 324 new accounts.
- Served as Account Manager for prestigious law firm account. Helped generate approximately $500,000 per month in new assets.
- Awarded President's Key Contributor Stock Options. This nomination was presented by Managers to employees for their contributions to the success of their respective departments.
- Nominated by the Manager of National Business Development for prestigious Canada Trade Brokers Excellence in Service Award – Team and Individual categories – for providing high-quality service to both clients and staff.
- Represented the sales team at The Investor Forum and The Financial Forum in Toronto.
- Gathered and assessed prospect/client financial needs in order to match company products and services.

SURREY INVESTMENT MANAGEMENT INC.   **1994 – 1998**
Client Service Representative (Contract position)

- Consistently met or exceeded call quota while maintaining a high level of client service.
- Provided prompt, courteous service regarding inquiries for product and administrative information.
- Established and maintained performance standards to increase productivity and client satisfaction.

Previous Financial Services Experience:

MYERS FINANCIAL CORP.
Client Service Representative (Contract position)

THE NEW WORLD BANK
Bank Teller

PROFESSIONAL DEVELOPMENT AND EDUCATION

LICENSES: Investment Representative (Ontario)   2002

CANADIAN SECURITIES INSTITUTE:
Investment Management Techniques Course   In Progress
Investment Representative Course   2001
Conducts and Practices Handbook   2000
Canadian Securities Course   2000

McGILL UNIVERSITY
Bachelor of Science – Biology   1992

COMPUTER SKILLS

- Windows 98/2000/NT, Novell GroupWise
- Netscape Communicator, Internet Explorer
- Microsoft Office, Corel Office, MS Outlook, Outlook Express
- Reuters Canpros, Starquote, PalTrak, FundServ, Dataphile
- Siebel eBusiness CRM, Business Objects

6 Functional Resume Samples

F ollowing are 16 sample functional resumes that you can use to get ideas for how to write and design your own winning resume. These are actual resumes of ex-offenders from prisons throughout the United States, although the names, addresses, phone numbers, and other personal information has been changed to protect each person's privacy.

Examples as Learning Tools

Our examples function as learning tools for understanding how each section of a functional resume should be designed and written for job seekers with different goals, interests, skills, experiences, and accomplishments. Remember, most employers are busy people who may spend no more than 30 seconds reviewing a single resume! A resume must both catch and hold the reader's attention if it is to become a serious effort at getting a job interview.

Pay particular attention to both the form and content of each resume. What exactly grabs and holds the attention of the reader in each case? **Form** includes such elements as format, design, headings, typestyles, highlighting, and use of white space. Form deals with many of the cosmetic elements that make a resume attractive or pleasing to the eye – gives it "curb appeal" — even before the reader has a chance to read each section of the resume.

On the other hand, **content** deals with messages being communicated through specific words and phrases. A resume should clearly communicate, through the choice of words and phrases, what a candidate has done, can do, and will do in the future. Employers look for cues, both positive and negative, of future performance in their organization. They look for possible red flags that could eliminate you from further consideration. Those red flags come in many different forms – misspelled words, poor grammar, major time gap, lack of relevant education and experience, and things you should never put on your resume, such as salary information, references, and personal information.

Using Our Examples Wisely

As you examine our examples, keep in mind how you plan to write each section of **your** resume. While you should never copy the content of someone else's resume, you can copy the form and creatively "borrow" content from our examples by adopting many of the principles incorporated in our resumes. You can do this by:

- Copying formats and designs that you like.
- Using similar headings and typestyles.
- Selecting words in job descriptions that match what you did at a similar job.
- Creating similar wording in skills summaries that coincide with your own skills.
- Getting ideas for how to highlight your training, degrees, certifications, and licenses.
- Developing "short stories" about each of your skills and experiences that you can communicate verbally when networking and interviewing for a job.

In the end, your resume should be based on sound writing principles and strategy, as well as be employer-oriented and reflect the real you. Learn from our examples, but write your own resume based on information about yourself.

Our Winning Cast of Characters

To understand why these resumes were written and designed the way that they were, read the following information about each one as you review it.

Resume:	**Leslie Monroe**, page 105
Prison:	2003 to Present (early 2006 release)
Writer:	Elizabeth Crimi, Maryland Correctional Institution for Women

Objective: Position in Hospitality or Retail

Strategy: Excellent example of how to prepare a resume for an individual with very limited work experience. Begins with clear statement of objective so anyone reviewing her resume will know precisely the type of job she is seeking. Follows with summary of personal skills and attributes, and then a short paragraph detailing her only work experience. Education section boosted with training she's attended in prison through the Maryland State Department of Education.

Resume: **Lucy Caldwell**, page 106

Prison: 2002 to Present (Summer 2006 release)

Writer: Elizabeth Crimi, Maryland Correctional Institution for Women

Objective: Position as a Cashier or Waitress

Strategy: Another excellent example of a resume format that works well for an individual with very limited and/or short-term work experience. Follows format of preceding resume, beginning with objective and skills, followed by brief listing of work experience (with no dates), and finally her education (her two training programs from prison and her prior college experience).

Resume: **Yolanda DaSilva**, page 107

Prison: 1999 to 2004

Writer: Melanie Noonan, Peripheral Pro, Inc.

Objective: Entry-level management position in the supermarket industry

Strategy: Highlight years of experience in key areas of supermarket operations to demonstrate broad-based experience and to draw attention to the number of years of experience she has. Work experience briefly summarized at end of resume to show steady work history (despite five-year break in employment).

Resume: **Lyndon Masters**, page 108

Prison: 1975 to Present

Writer: Jane Roqueplot, JaneCo's Sensible Solutions

Objective: Position as a Cook, Laborer, Janitor, Barber, or Machine Operator

Strategy: Resume begins with detailed summary to highlight all of his relevant skills as they relate to the different positions he will be pursuing as he makes the transition out of prison after 30 years. All work experience presented on resume were jobs he held while incarcerated with companies that contracted with the prison. Note that there is no indication of his age (52) since dates for education and training were omitted and no early experience was included.

Resume:	**Virginia Nagel**, page 109
Prison:	2004 to Present (late 2006 release)
Writer:	Gina Taylor, Gina Taylor & Associates
Objective:	Position as a Landscaper
Strategy:	Focus of resume is on skills acquired through education which tie directly to his current job objective. Detailed information included about specific classes, projects, activities, and volunteer contributions. Employment history includes current position while incarcerated (listed as Kansas Air National Guard) as well as prior experience to show a semi-stable work history.

Resume:	**Michael James**, page 110
Prison:	2002 to 2004
Writer:	Beth Woodworth, Job Training Center of Tehama County
Objective:	Undecided; open to numerous opportunities
Strategy:	This resume showcases his experience in management/supervision, medical/counseling, and customer service so that he can use the resume for a diversity of job openings. The bulleted format allows for a quick review of skills and qualifications. Work experience presented in a unique format (1995 to Present) so that his period of incarceration (2002 to 2004) would not be noticeable.

Resume:	**Warren L. Tweed**, page 111
Prison:	2002 to 2005
Writer:	Melanie Noonan, Peripheral Pro, LLC
Objective:	Position as a Landscaper or Groundskeeper
Strategy:	Detailed capabilities section clearly and comprehensively highlights all of his experience in horticulture, grounds maintenance, and equipment operation (2/3 of the resume). Clearly positions him as a well-qualified candidate for his job objective. Next sec-

tion, Related Experience, only includes his position as a Maintenance Worker (while incarcerated) which is directly related to his current goal. Prior experience briefly mentioned to show a solid eight-year record of employment.

Resume:	**Delores Evert**, page 112
Prison:	2002 to 2005
Writer:	Louise Garver, Career Directions, LLC
Objective:	Position in Electronic Assembly
Strategy:	Clean and concise presentation beginning with a brief objective and followed with a short, hard-hitting summary of related qualifications. Experience section is utilized to present in-depth information about the skills and technical qualifications she has. Employment briefly mentioned at the end with dates, including her position with Stanley Corporation (contracted with local prison) while incarcerated.

Resume:	**Matthew McIntyre**, page 113
Prison:	2003 to Present (January 2006 release)
Writer:	Teena Rose, Resume to Referral
Objective:	Position in the Real Estate field
Strategy:	Three-quarters of resume dedicated to his experience, administrative skills, training, and licenses in the real estate industry. Resume clearly positions him as a well-qualified candidate for an entry-level administrative assignment. Note that much of his real estate training was completed while incarcerated. Only includes a very brief listing of actual work experience, prior to his incarceration, to showcase his 11-year stable career with one employer (a great selling point for any job seeker).

Resume:	**Annette Lewiston**, page 114
Prison:	1989 to 1999
Writer:	Ellen Mulqueen, The Institute of Living
Objective:	Position as a Certified Nurses' Aide
Strategy:	Detailed summary demonstrating all relevant qualifications, followed by education section which draws visual attention to recent CNA program and honors graduation. Experience briefly summarized at end to show track record of employment even

though not relevant to current job objective. Jobs with State of Connecticut demonstrate 10-year employment record with one organization without disclosing her prison record.

Resume:	**Valerie Smith**, page 115
Prison:	2005
Writer:	Melanie Noonan, Peripheral Pro, LLC
Objective:	Position as a Nursing Assistant
Strategy:	"Traditional" functional resume used to highlight the strength of her experience in nursing and patient care. Clean and concise summary allows reader to instantly understand the type of position she is seeking, educational credentials follow to support that, and then a detailed summary of her relevant skills further demonstrates her abilities. Brief mention of employment experience includes position while imprisoned (Kitchen Assistant, Brookline C.F.), but does not disclose that she was incarcerated.

Resume:	**Alice Ashman**, page 116
Prison:	2003 to 2005
Writer:	Lee Anne Grundish, Grafix Services, Etc.
Objective:	Position as a Dental Assistant
Strategy:	Resumes focuses almost exclusively on what she has accomplished while in prison, although the fact that she was incarcerated is never disclosed. Unique and attractive format draws immediate attention to the resume and then captures a reader's interest with strong presentation of her credentials, education, lab experience, and internships. Resume also includes her work experience as a Health Center Clerk, but, again, does not disclose that she was an inmate. Resume presents an extremely well-qualified Dental Assistant ready for her first professional assignment.

Resume:	**Henry R. Lewis**, page 117
Prison:	2004 to Present (late 2006 release)
Writer:	Wendy Enelow, Enelow Enterprises, Inc.
Objective:	Position in Network Engineering or Technical Support
Strategy:	Headline format clearly states career goal and is substantiated by an excellent summary of his qualifications, educational credentials, and technical skills and certifications. To draw attention away

from his actual history of work experience, accomplishments are presented first in a separate section. Jobs are then listed, with no dates, to demonstrate that he has practical work experience, the most recent of which is related to his current career goal.

Resume: **George A. McNally**, page 118
Prison: 2003 to 2005
Writer: Andrea Howard, NYS Department of Labor
Objective: Position working with, counseling, and supporting at-risk youth
Strategy: Excellent functional resume presentation beginning with clearly stated career goal and followed by an extensive summary of his skills and qualifications across a broad range of related functions. Education also presented in detail, along with specific coursework related to his current objective. Brief listing of work experience presented at the end, including his position as a Program Assistant at the Coxsackie Correctional Facility (will be interpreted as a "paid position" and not a "prison job").

Resume: **Hank Christo**, page 119-120
Prison: 1998 to 2004
Writer: Brian Leeson, Vector Consultants Pty. Ltd.
Objective: Position as a Health Issues Educator
Strategy: The entire first page of this resume focuses on the unique skills, qualifications, competencies, and achievements of his career in health education and peer education. Including specific achievements on the first page strengthens resume presentation and immediately communicates a message that he delivers results. Page two briefly mentions his work experience (including his four years as a Seminar Presenter and HIV Educator while incarcerated). Employers will interpret this as professional work experience and not a period of incarceration, which can be disclosed during an interview.

Resume: **Jack E. Morrow**, page 121-122
Prison: 2004 to 2005
Writer: Michael Davis, The Michaels Group
Objective: Position as a Crisis Intervention or Community Relations Specialist

Strategy: Another outstanding presentation of a functional resume where all of page one focuses on his qualifications, skills, and achievements. This resume creates a strong picture of an individual well-qualified for his chosen career goal. Page two is then used to briefly mention his work experience and his impressive educational credentials. No mention is made of the fact that he can no longer work in a church or hospital as a result of his imprisonment – the reason for his career change.

LESLIE MONROE

8921 Martinsburg Parkway
Big Island, Virginia 25367
434-908-8761

OBJECTIVE

Seeking employment in the hospitality or retail field.

SKILLS

Good people skills; helpful, and friendly.
Ambitious, outgoing, energetic, and self-confident.
Good manual speed and dexterity.
Responsible, dependable, analytical, fair-minded, and detail-oriented.

EXPERIENCE

Three years' experience providing basic home health care for woman who needed
regular insulin and dialysis treatments. Assisted patient with personal needs,
including administering insulin. Provided housekeeping and child care services as
needed.

EDUCATION

Maryland Department of Education   Baltimore, Maryland
GED Program – Currently Enrolled   2005 to Present

Maryland Department of Education   Jessup, Maryland
Career Exploration Certificate (105 hours)   2005

REFERENCES

Available Upon Request

LUCY CALDWELL
562 Clay Street
Baltimore, Maryland 21229
990-892-3821

OBJECTIVE

Position as a Cashier or Waitress.

SKILLS

Experienced in operating a cash register and lottery machine.
Highly motivated and reliable.
Work well with people.
Excellent communication skills.
Good manual speed and dexterity.

EXPERIENCE

Five years' experience as a Cashier. Employers included:

Caldor
Smith's Liquors
Milano's Supermarket
Dresser Industries

EDUCATION

Maryland Department of Education Secondary Education Program	Baltimore, Maryland Currently enrolled
Maryland Department of Education Career Exploration Certificate (105 hours)	Jessup, Maryland 2003
Community College of Baltimore General Studies (20 credits)	Baltimore, Maryland 1998 to 1999

References Available Upon Request

Yolanda DaSilva

(602) 566-2390   84-14 Doremus Avenue ♦ Tucson, AZ 95726

Past experience in various SUPERMARKET positions that shows a strong desire to contribute to efficiency and better customer relations.

WORK HABITS
- Fast learner
- Punctual
- Team player

- Honest and trustworthy
- Good attendance record
- Willing to help in any area

EXPERIENCE

Salad Bar Attendant (4 years)
- Maintained fresh, appealing, and well-stocked displays of over 30 separate items.
- Followed recipes precisely for consistent quality of specially mixed salads.
- Kept counters, hoods, utensils, and surrounding floor area clean and free of debris.

Deli Server (6 years)
- Waited on numerous customers during busy lunch hours.
- Safely operated cold-cut slicing machine at various settings according to customers' orders.
- Suggested related items to increase sales.
- Assembled attractive party trays which brought in considerable repeat business.

Meat Wrapper (2 years)
- Accurately weighed, packaged, and priced over 20 different types and cuts of meat and seafood daily.
- Assisted in butchering area with preparation of chicken parts and ground meat.
- Processed customers' special requests.

Cashier (5 years)
- Efficiently handled transactions consisting of any combination of cash, checks, credit card payments, food stamps, and coupon deductions. Always maintained accurately balanced register drawer.
- Won incentive awards for speed scanning.
- Correctly rang up unusual fruits and vegetables and identified such for other cashiers.

EMPLOYMENT

APEX CONVENIENCE MARKET, Santa Cruz, AZ	2004–Present
SUPER SAVER MARKET, Tucson, AZ	1995–1999
FOOD KING SUPERSTORE, Tucson, AZ	1993–1995
GONZALEZ FINE FOODS, Nogales, Mexico	1990–1992

LYNDON MASTERS

1614 Sample Road
Franklin, Pennsylvania 16323
Home: (814) 674-3325
Cell: (814) 601-5252

SUMMARY OF APTITUDES

Prep Cook · General Laborer · Janitor · Barber · Machine Operator

➢ Responsible, easygoing individual; focus on being positive force in workplace. Persistent and persevering in approach to achieving goals.

➢ Work capably and skillfully with hands as well as with hand tools and machines to perform job. Concerned about quality of work.

➢ Understand and carefully follow instructions. Comprehensive in problem solving. Logical, objective approach serves as "anchor of reality." Adhere to company policy.

➢ Dependable, steady team member. People-oriented; build good relationships. Work well with people from diverse backgrounds and cultures.

➢ Skilled in use of a variety of machines and equipment:
  - ✓ Steel industry machinery
  - ✓ Stitching machine
  - ✓ Packaging equipment
  - ✓ Floor care equipment
  - ✓ Boring machine
  - ✓ Presser
  - ✓ Hairstyling and hair care
  - ✓ Painting tools
  - ✓ Lay machine
  - ✓ Paint and dye machine
  - ✓ Landscaping tools
  - ✓ Commercial dishwasher

RECENT EMPLOYMENT

ASSEMBLER / GENERAL LABOR, Canon Metals – Franklin, PA	*2003 – Present*
SECURITY / GENERAL LABOR, Derek's Restaurant & Grille – Franklin, PA	*2002 – 2003*
MACHINE OPERATOR, Hampton Machinery – Wampum, PA	*2000 – 2001*
KITCHEN WORKER, part time, City Hospital – Oil City, PA	*2000 – 2001*
GENERAL LABORER, part time, Lakeside Gardens – Franklin, PA	*2000 – 2001*
JANITOR, Doug's Janitorial Services – Oil City, PA	*2000*

EDUCATION / CONTINUING EDUCATION / TRAINING

Liberal Arts Coursework, 2 years, University of Indiana
Certificate, Barber, Commonwealth of Pennsylvania
Machinery Apprenticeship
Inventory and Stock Management
Stress and Anger Management

VALUES TO THE ORGANIZATION

(Based on professional behavioral assessments)
Defines, clarifies, gets information, criticizes and tests · Accurate · Intuitive · Patient · Empathetic

VIRGINIA NAGEL

22 Grisolm Lane • Latrobe, KS 38992
757-388-2983

LANDSCAPING

Trained in all aspects of landscaping maintenance and installation,
working under the supervision of degreed horticulturist.

EDUCATION

GENERAL EDUCATION DIPLOMA, 2005   TOPEKA, KANSAS

HORTICULTURE, LANDSCAPING, AND GREENHOUSE SKILLS

- MARKETING GARDENER
- BEDDING PLANTS
- PLANT SCIENCE
- BULBS
- COMPOSTING
- PRUNING
- TURF
- TURF RENOVATION

- MUM PRODUCTION
- INDOOR PLANTS
- GREENHOUSE OPERATIONS
- GREENHOUSE CONSTRUCTION
- EQUIPMENT OPERATIONS
- RESEARCH & SELF-STUDY
- BASIC DRAFTING
- HUMAN RELATIONS

COURSES AND VOLUNTEER ACTIVITIES

- PATHWAYS TO POSITIVE RELATIONS
- STOP VIOLENCE
- PARENTING
- NUTRITIONAL EDUCATION

- POOCHES AND PALS
- GIRL SCOUTS BEYOND BARS
- UNITED METHODIST WOMEN'S GROUP
- NATIVE AMERICAN CULTURE GROUP

EMPLOYMENT HISTORY

ROADS AND GROUNDS MAINTENANCE   *02/05 - CURRENTLY*
KANSAS AIR NATIONAL GUARD (TCF)   TOPEKA, KANSAS

Mow, plant, seed, trim, prune, paint, mulch, and recycle. Trained to operate Hustler 3400
industrial mower, weed eaters, gas trimmers, pole trimmers, and industrial snow-blower.

BREAK CREW ASSISTANT   *03/03 - 09/04*
TONY'S PIZZA SERVICE   SALINA, KANSAS

Provided break coverage for all associates in areas of packaging, processing, bakery, and
freezer line operations.

CUSTODIAL SANITATION ASSISTANT   *6/02 - 12/02*
SALINA REGIONAL HEALTH CARE /HOSPITAL   SALINA, KANSAS

Cleaned rooms after surgeries and after patients were released, sanitizing before, during, and
after care was given to patients.

Michael James   333 South Main St. # 2D · Sacramento, CA 95824
916-200-5123

PERSONAL PROFILE

- Team player with excellent ability to work independently.
- Detail oriented, even in a fast-paced environment.
- Strong skills in conflict resolution and crisis intervention.
- Successfully work with and supervise diverse people in a variety of situations.

PROFESSIONAL HIGHLIGHTS

Management/Supervision
- 12 years' experience in management positions in retail, medical, and warehousing.
- Supervised up to 7 employees in a department.
- Responsibilities included but not limited to:
  - Daily operations; opening/closing; weekly/monthly ordering; shipping/receiving.
  - Scheduling and evaluations of staff.
  - Monitoring supplies, merchandise, and cash flow.
  - Solving customer complaints and addressing grievances at local level.

Medical/Counseling
- Informed and counseled individuals regarding medical test results (including AIDS).
- Coordinated group activities for mentally ill residents.
- Performed, processed, and logged medical lab procedures on patients including:
  - Blood and arterial draws.
  - Urinalysis.
  - Vitals - blood pressure, temperature, respiratory rate, and heart rate.

Customer Service
- Over 15 years providing direct service to the public.
- Extremely reliable, hard-working, and honest.
- Outstanding performance working with shoppers, sellers, retailers, wholesalers, doctors, researchers, patients, and disgruntled customers.

WORK EXPERIENCE *from 1995 to Present*

House Supervisor	Main Street Homeless Shelter	Sacramento, CA
Cook	Tony's Pizza	Sacramento, CA
Phlebotomist	El Centro Pathology	Los Angeles, CA
Lab Assistant	Los Angeles Hospital	Los Angeles, CA
Lab Assistant Manager	L.V. Plasma	Las Vegas, NV
Shipping & Receiving	RTM Corporation	Las Vegas, NV

EDUCATION

Med Tech Certificate	Los Angeles Community College	Los Angeles, CA

WARREN L. TWEED

P.O. Box 673, Youngstown, OH 44501
Message Phone: (216) 555-5555

Position Desired: Landscaper/Groundskeeper

CAPABILITIES:

Horticulture
- Broad knowledge of planting and care techniques for a large array of plant materials including:
  - florals and decorative herbaceous plants (annuals and perennials).
  - deciduous and evergreen trees and shrubs.
  - grass and sod.
- Strong awareness of factors affecting viability (soil, water, sunlight, and seasonal conditions) enabling optimal placement and growth.
- Recognition of early symptoms and application of preventive measures for plant diseases and insect control.

Grounds Maintenance
- Understanding of topography and drainage plans at sites such as golf courses, botanical gardens, and commercial parks where attractive settings are required.
- Ability to develop new landscaping arrangements as well as follow all stages of existing landscape plans.
- Diligent in keeping up with turf maintenance schedules in the areas of fertilization, irrigation, weeding, and mowing.
- Pesticide applicator's license pending.

Equipment Operation
- Skilled in the safe handling and maintenance of various groundskeeping equipment including:

— mowers	— tractors	— wood chippers
— spreaders	— edgers	— leaf/debris blowers
— trimmers	— sprayers	— watering systems
— rototillers	— chain saws	— snow-removal machines

RELATED EXPERIENCE:

State of Ohio, Youngstown, OH (2002–2005)
MAINTENANCE WORKER, PARKS AND PUBLIC LANDS
- Began as member of cleanup crew while continuing professional development. Advanced to higher levels of responsibility after acquiring skills in the planting of many types of herbaceous materials and the maintenance of formal gardens, trees, and shrubs.

PRIOR EXPERIENCE:

Hayden Griswold Corporation, Salem, OH (1991–1999)
ACCOUNTING MANAGER

EDUCATION:

Mahoning County Community College Extension Center, Youngstown, OH (2001–2003)
Courses: Turf & Landscape Maintenance; Irrigation Design; Basics of Landscape Design

Ohio State University — B.S. Accounting (1990)

Delores Evert
89 Forest Street
West Milton, OH 45383
(937) 698-4490 ▪▪ EvertD@aol.com

Objective: Electronic Assembly

Summary

Offering 15 years of experience in electronic assembly. Proficient in sub and final assembly, test, and inspection of electronic components, including printed circuit boards, wiring, and other products.

Skilled in operating various hand tools and computerized machinery, including assembling and handling simple to complex production operations.

Experience

Electronic Assembly/Machining

- Assembled and built printed circuit boards and automotive parts (exhaust and intake for Chrysler cars) from blueprints/schematics, using soldering iron, gages, and various other hand tools.
- Operated exhaust machine and made minor repairs/adjustments to Bradley Allen computer to maintain production goals and minimize down time.

Team Leadership

- Selected by management as lead person on Cybex production line, overseeing team of 16 assemblers.
- Provided training, guidance, and ongoing support to assembly team members to achieve company productivity goals.

Quality Control/Shipping & Receiving

- Inspected over 340 boxes of electronic parts each day to ensure compliance to company standards.
- Recorded incoming and outgoing shipments as well as prepared items for shipment; verified information against bills of lading, invoices, orders, and other records.

Employment History

STANLEY CORPORATION, Dayton, OH (2002 to 2005)
Quality Control Inspector

SULVANA WIRE COMPANY, Dayton, OH (1995 to 2002)
Electronic Assembler

NEW VISIONS, Dayton, OH (1990 to 1995)
Electronic Assembler

Education

Electronics Technology courses
Dayton Community College, Dayton, OH

MATTHEW MCINTYRE

12581 ½ E. High Street, Springfield, OH 45504
Home: (937) 321-1844 | Cell: (937) 228-1833
M_McIntyre@springfield.net

ENTRY-LEVEL ADMINISTRATIVE ASSISTANT TO THE REAL ESTATE FIELD
Assist with property analysis, escrow, open houses, and records management.

- Possess the ground-floor skills to perform an array of RE office tasks, from assisting realtors with special projects and answering incoming inquiries to maintaining property documentation and scheduling.

- Serve as the "right hand" for a realtor; assisting with property listings, creating a synchronized schedule, and helping with showing properties.

- Schedule and coordinate local and national travel arrangements for one or several realtors, concentrating on prompt arrival and cost-effective options.

- Knowledgeable of RE jargon and terminology.

- Assist realtors with developing new prospects and handling marketing projects designed to draw repeat and referral clients.

- Correspond professionally between buyers and sellers, along with other agencies such as mortgage brokers, records offices, and financial institutions.

ADMINISTRATIVE CAPABILITIES

Ideal support position would encompass:

Inbound Call Assistance · Administrative Support · Office Management
Order Fulfillment · Client Communications · Project Completion
Customer Satisfaction · Management Liaison · Efficiency Improvements
Records Management · Executive Officer Support · Problem Solving

EDUCATION & SOFTWARE

Real Estate Trading Services License, 2005 *(awaiting test date)*
University of Dayton, Dayton, OH
Program encompassed sales/sales management, real property law, licensing system, estate/co-ownership issues, land registration, liability, tenancies/arbitration/termination, financial logistics, contractual documents, financing, taxes, and cost analysis.

Fast-Track Real Estate Tutorials, 2004
5-week Tutorial Course

MS Word, Excel, Outlook, Windows 2000/XP, Internet/Research

PROFESSIONAL EXPERIENCE

THE COMMUNITY HOSPITAL, SPRINGFIELD, OH

DIETARY AIDE, DEPARTMENT OF FOOD AND NUTRITION, 1994–2003

- Verified and distributed meals for patients admitted to the extended care unit, which included the preparation of foods based on certain diet restrictions and delivery based on meal schedules.

- Communicated with nurses, doctors, and other medical staff to ensure patients were provided with accurate food and nutrition.

DISTRIBUTION CLERK, 1992–1994

- Distributed equipment, linens, and other supplies, to various departments and floors throughout the hospital. Transported patients.

ANNETTE LEWISTON

104 Irving Place
Springfield Massachusetts 01109
413.555.9876

CERTIFIED NURSES' AIDE

- ❑ Completed CNA Program with honors.
- ❑ Strong and energetic, with good interpersonal skills.
- ❑ Intelligent; worked as literacy volunteer and math tutor.
- ❑ Solid customer service experience.
- ❑ Fast learner, eager to develop new competencies.
- ❑ Dependable, honest, open-minded, and comfortable with diverse populations.
- ❑ Computer skills include Word, Excel, Access, PowerPoint, and PageMaker.

EDUCATION

Springfield Technical Community College, Springfield, MA
CNA Program – Honors Graduate   2003-2005

Three Rivers Community College, New London, CT
Completed several business and liberal arts courses.

EXPERIENCE

Stop & Shop Supermarket, Springfield, MA   2000 – 2003
Various positions: Cashier, Florist Shop, Customer Service, Dairy Stock
- ❑ Excellent work history. Rotate to different departments as needed.

State of Connecticut, Niantic, CT   1989 – 1999
Various positions: Cook, Prep Cook, Commercial Cleaner, Painter, Electrician Assistant.

Valerie Smith

636 Archibald Street * Boston, Massachusetts 09809 * 617-555-1212

OCCUPATIONAL GOAL: **Nursing Assistant** in private home or long-term care facility.

EDUCATION

Suffolk County Community College, Boston, MA
Certified Nursing Assistant course, 2005

Walt Whitman High School, Boston, MA
General Diploma, 2002

SKILLS

Health Care
> ➤ Volunteered at a nursing home for 2 years.
> ➤ Delivered and served meals to up to 15 patients.
> ➤ Made up beds.
> ➤ Assisted patients with bathing and grooming.
> ➤ Took and recorded temperatures.
> ➤ Transported wheelchair-bound patients.

Homemaking
> ➤ Cared for 75-year old grandmother who was diabetic and visually impaired.
> ➤ Performed housekeeping tasks that included cooking, cleaning, and laundry.
> ➤ Shopped for food and prepared special diet.
> ➤ Administered insulin injections.
> ➤ Served as visual guide.

Food Service
> ➤ Experienced in cooking and food preparation for a medium-sized institution.
> ➤ Learned and practiced food handling and sanitation procedures.
> ➤ Helped to serve meals to approximately 125 residents.
> ➤ Prepared food for special occasion banquets.

Customer Relations
> ➤ Greeted patrons and filled their orders at a fast-food restaurant.
> ➤ Entered sales and gave correct change.

EMPLOYMENT

Brookline C.F., Brookline, MA   2005
  Kitchen Assistant

Pleasant Valley Nursing Home, Boston, MA   2003–2005
  Volunteer Orderly

McDonald's, Boston, MA   2001–2002
  Order Taker/Cashier

Alice Ashman

2948 Peru Street
Toledo, Ohio 43612
(419) 888-2482

Profile

A motivated, quality-oriented professional with a solid base of career preparation and training as a Dental Assistant: familiarity with dental procedures, chair-side techniques, and office skills, and a commitment to provide quality dental care and services.

Credentials

- **DENTAL ASSISTANT CERTIFICATION**
- **RADIOGRAPHY (X-RAY) CERTIFICATION**

Education

DENTAL ASSISTING CERTIFICATE, *State of Ohio Vocational Training Program*   2005
- Successfully completed intensive 6-month program.
- *Areas of Study*:
  - **General Dentistry** • **Periodontics** • **Orthodontics** • **Endodontics** • **Pediatric Dentistry**
  - **Oral and Maxillofacial Surgery** • **Oral Pathology** • **Fixed and Removable Prostodontics**
  - **Pain Management / Anxiety** • **Chair-Side Restorative Materials** • **Pharmacology** • **Sterilization**
  - **Office / Clerical Functions: Business Management / Administration** • **Ethics and Jurisprudence**

RADIOGRAPHY TRAINING, *State of Ohio Vocational Training Program*   2005

Dental Laboratory Experience

- **Alginate Impressions** • **Pouring / Trimming Models** • **Preparing Whitening Trays and Provisionals**
- **Acrylic Resin Custom Trays** • **Bite Registrations** • **Polysulfide Impressions** • **Fluoride Application**
- **Adapting, Trimming and Seating Custom Temporary Restorations** • **Placement of Dental Dams**

Dental Internship

DENTAL ASSISTANT INTERN, *Dr. David Jones, State of Ohio*   2004–2005
- *Chair-Side Assistant* for dental surgeries.
- *Experience:*
  - **Composites** • **Extractions** • **Sealants** • **Amalgams** • **Radiographs (X-Ray)**
  - **Seated Stainless Steel Crowns** • **Assembly of Tofflemire Matrix Bands**
  - **Implants** • **Bindings** • **X-Rays** • **Sterilization** • **Patient Charting**
  - **Patient Education in Total Dental Care and Preventive Maintenance**

Employment Experience

HEALTH CENTER CLERK, *State of Ohio*   2003–2005
- *Receptionist:* Scheduled appointments and greeted patients.
- *Records Management:* Maintained confidentiality and accuracy in updating charts and filing information. Ensured adherence to regulatory standards and guidelines, including HIPAA (Health Insurance Portability and Accountability Act).
- *Physician Attendant:* Prepared examination rooms and equipment. Assisted doctors in administering health care treatments and procedures.

HENRY R. LEWIS

12 Spruce Lake Street
Milwaukee, WI 59802

(211) 981-6273
glover@msn.com

NETWORK ENGINEERING/TECHNICAL SUPPORT

SUMMARY OF QUALIFICATIONS

- Solutions-driven network engineer providing technical support to improve performance, operational efficiencies, and expense reduction.
- Flexible and focused, with unique analytical problem-solving ability.
- Solid theoretical knowledge of computer and network architecture and Microsoft Operating System.
- Excellent communication, team-building, and conflict-management skills.

EDUCATION

Caldwell County Community College, Lewiston, WI

Network Engineer: Windows NT, Darnell Technologies, Ada, WI

Networking & Information Technology Certifications:

MCSE	**Workstation**	**Windows 95**
MCP+I	**NT Server/Enterprise**	**Windows 3.x**
A+ Certified	**Networking Essentials**	**Windows NT**
Microsoft NT	**Windows NT Server 4.0**	**Internet Info-Server**
MS DOS 6.22	**TCP/IP Implementation**	**Internet Explorer 5.0**

ACCOMPLISHMENTS

- Resolved security issues on Windows NT involving group account policies and end users.
- Engineered effective Windows NT security structure and implementation in working networks.
- Implemented and routed network around TCP/IP protocol suite.
- Performed diagnostics, myriad configurations, and peripheral repairs.
- Installed software, provided peer-to-peer technical support, and consulted on LAN development.

WORK HISTORY

Computer Technician, Crisp Electronics, Lewiston, WI

Equipment Operator, Martinsville Building, Lewiston, WI

Carpenter, Dove Home Builders, Craigmont, WI

George A. McNally

1303 Providence Run Street   518.441.2927   Albany, NY 12207
                                     gam@aol.com

Career Goal

A take-charge individual with a strong desire to help **at-risk youth** succeed. Offering counseling experience to an agency that specializes in adolescent employability and recovery.

Summary of Skills

Two years experience working with adults on substance abuse, self worth and life purpose. Assisted in the facilitation of group counseling programs where decisions relating to vocational training, personal, and family issues were the focus. Expressed empathy and compassion to participants while teaching through self experience.

Served as a counselor's aide in a program serving at-risk youth. Concentrated on helping youth stay on the right path by focusing on life issues, decision-making, and goal setting.

➤ Areas of knowledge include:

Assessment Administration and Interpretation	Career Decision Making And Employability
Peer Troubles	Drug Addiction
Physical And Emotional Scars	Domestic Violence
Establishment of Life Goals	Pregnancy And Sexuality
Business Development And Budgeting	Role Playing and Mediation

Formal Academic Training

Hudson Valley Community College ~ Troy, NY ~ 1996-1997
Human Services

➤ Related Classes:

   Child and Adolescent Psychology; Counseling; Chemical Dependency; Career Counseling and Assessments

Automotive High School ~ Brooklyn NY ~ 1995
HS Diploma ~ Auto Body Repair

Employment History

Program Assistant ~ Coxsackie Correctional Facility ~ Coxsackie, NY ~ 2003-2005
Club Support ~ Night Moves Club ~ Albany, NY ~ 1999-2000
Warehouse / Labor ~ Best Temporary Employment Agency ~ Albany, NY ~ 1998-2000
Group Aide ~ Teen Action Association ~ Waterford, NY ~ 1997-1998

HANK CHRISTO

Telephone: (03) 9808 4100

25 College Street
West Melbourne, Victoria, Australia 3003

EMPLOYMENT OBJECTIVE

Health Issues Educator

CAREER SUMMARY

Peer educator trained to counsel and advise on safe sex, substance abuse, and HIV, Four years' experience presenting seminars to school students and delivering individual counseling to youth and adults at risk. Personal life experience has reinforced my ability to achieve particular empathy with young and adult offenders, ex-offenders, and those at risk of offending or re-offending. Experienced in planning and presenting educational seminars to schools, community groups, and prison communities.

KEY COMPETENCIES

- Communicating • Liaising • Planning and Organizing • Networking
- Behavioral Management • Presenting • Facilitating • Counseling

COMPETENCY APPLICATIONS

- Counseling before and after HIV testing.
- Planning and organizing seminars on personal health topics – HIV risk, safe sex, substance and alcohol abuse, behavior management.
- Advising on Universal Infection Control.
- Presenting challenging health topics to groups of school students.
- Assessing risk behaviors and situations.
- Establishing and maintaining small in-house libraries on health issues.
- Networking and liaising with similar organizations for resource sharing.

RELATED ACHIEVEMENTS

- Organized and presented seminars on health-risk issues to high-school students and community groups. Received excellent feedback, including requests for annual repeats.

- Upgraded and maintained the Health Issues Section of a prison library through networking with information agencies and locating/downloading Internet material.

- Initiated networking between individual prison health committees statewide, achieving resource sharing. Structured educational programs for inmates.

RELATED EXPERIENCE

Volunteer
Aids Council of Victoria   2004–present

Seminar Presenter and HIV Peer Educator
Department of Correctional Service, Victoria   2000–2004

RELATED EDUCATION AND TRAINING

Volunteer Training
Aids Council of Victoria   2004

Counseling Strategies
Center for Personal Relationships, Victoria   2004

Certificate in HIV Counseling
Peer Education Training, Melbourne, Victoria   2000

Jack E. Morrow

6175 Highberry Ct., Clayton, NC 27520
Phone: (919) 844-2943   jackm26@prodigy.net

Crisis Intervention / Community Relations Specialist

Ordained minister seeks challenging opportunity to apply broad-based skills in training, counseling, advising, leadership, mediation, and crisis intervention to improve the quality of life for those in need.

QUALIFICATIONS

- Counseling
- Crisis Intervention
- Teaching / Mentoring
- Project Development

- Group Facilitation
- Public Speaking
- Mediation / Conflict Resolution
- Creative Writing

SELECTED ACHIEVEMENTS

Co-founded and co-facilitated support group for cancer survivors and their families. Provided "safe place" to express feelings and receive support and education for both patients and families that created a "sounding board" to help cope with their illness and treatment.

Organized and implemented the first chaplaincy program at the Clayton, NC Squadron, Civil Air Patrol (USAF Auxiliary). Taught leadership classes, participated in search and rescue missions, and coordinated annual events helping to achieve the national directive.

Took initiative to help management confront hostile forces determined to unionize the medical center. Provided "words of encouragement" at the beginning of every managers' meeting plus counseled individual administrators and managers to help improve morale and dedication.

Chaired committee representing a consortium of pastoral care departments from the Greater Clayton, NC area. Provided educational opportunities and seminars for health care professionals on relevant topics resulting in cooperation instead of competition among healthcare institutions at the pastoral care level.

Led group of professional chaplains and served as North Carolina's resource person on matters pertaining to the national organization. Carried out national directives and tested new candidates seeking to become Board Certified Chaplains.

Established support group for heart surgery patients and their families. Met over coffee and talked about various heart procedures to help everyone cope with this medical crisis, to reduce anxiety and fear, and to give support at a difficult time.

Planned first Humor Committee. Since humor is good medicine, assembled multi-disciplinary committee to sponsor humor activities for employees, which resulted in reduced stress and improved morale.

Jack E. Morrow

PROFESSIONAL EXPERIENCE

St. Francis Medical Center, Clayton, North Carolina, 1988 – 2004

> **Director Spiritual Care Department,** 1994 - 2004
>
> **Associate Director, Spiritual Care Department,** 1992 - 1994
>
> **Staff Chaplain,** 1988 - 1992

Holly Hill Hospital, Clayton, North Carolina

> **Chaplain Resident,** 1987 - 1988

Omega Baptist Church, Clayton, North Carolina
> **Pastor,** 1983 - 1987

EDUCATION

Doctor of Ministry, United Theological Seminary
Clayton, North Carolina

Master of Divinity, Southeastern Baptist Theological Seminary
Wake Forest, North Carolina

Bachelor of Science, Piedmont Baptist College
Winston-Salem, North Carolina

7

Writing Powerful Cover Letters

E X-OFFENDERS ARE NO STRANGERS to letter writing. And they are no strangers to making numerous writing errors! Indeed, many understand the power of letters better than most people. Some of their most precious moments are when they receive letters from the outside. While incarcerated they also have time to write letters to family members and friends. Many learn the art of expressing themselves in writing – tell the truth, seek forgiveness, ask for help, formulate new goals, and dream about tomorrow. Some develop pen pal relationships, write for free assistance, deal with legal issues, or communicate with complete strangers. Others, who lack basic literacy and writing skills, may ask fellow inmates to help them write letters. They, too, know the importance of letters.

Questionable Inmate Writing Skills

But let's talk truth about what gets written in prison. Few inmates know how to write effective letters. In fact, prisons are often dens of prolific but bad letter writers. If you've been writing letters, don't assume you know how to write an effective letter. On the contrary, you may be your own worst enemy when it comes to writing letters – you express in writing why no one may want to hire you! Many strangers who receive unsolicited letters from ex-offenders throw them in the trash, because such letters violate so many basic rules of good letter writing. Therefore, this is probably a good time to re-evaluate your writing skills to make sure you are writing **perfect letters** that could possibly change your life.

Hope for a New Day

Effective letter writers learn how to maintain and develop relationships through correspondence. Many also experience a whole range of emotions through letters – joy, love, honesty, forgiveness, manipulation, rejection, and disappointment in not receiving replies to their letters. Most importantly, letters give them hope for a new and better day.

When you write letters in your job search, you also experience a full range of emotions, from high expectations for getting a positive reply to the disappointment and possible depression following silence and rejections. But the one common element running through the letter writing experience is one's ability to **persuade others to take action**. We're not talking about manipulation – just honest persuasion.

That's exactly what you want to do when writing letters during your job search – persuade others to assist you with your job search and get employers to invite you to a job interview and offer you a job. As such, letter writing should be a powerful exercise in getting others to take actions that lead to landing a job. To have the greatest impact, your letters must be well organized, error-free, honest, thoughtful, and purposeful. They must present an image of someone who is goal-oriented, truthful, and competent. Whatever you do, never neglect the importance of letter writing. It can well change your life!

Inmate Letter Writers

We make no assumptions about the literacy and education levels, housing situations, or behavior of our ex-offender audience. Indeed, we know, based on national literacy surveys, that over 50% of prisoners are either illiterate or exhibit marginal reading, writing, and math skills. We also know from other surveys that nearly 60% of ex-offenders remain unemployed and from 15 to 27 percent of prisoners expect to go into homeless shelters upon release. Furthermore, we know that 57% of federal and 70% of state inmates regularly used drugs before being incarcerated and that perhaps over 80% were using drugs and alcohol at or near the time of their arrest.

On the whole, our ex-offender population lacks many basic literacy and education skills that are key to writing effective letters that clearly express their skills, competencies, and goals. Many ex-offenders lack a stable address and may be tempted to once again abuse drugs and alcohol. And many continue to engage in the "art of the con," with letters designed to manipulate others through lies and deceit. Forewarned of such prison-based letter writers, many employers are reluctant to take such letter writers seriously. After all, this is not a pretty picture to confront if you are an employer who is aware of such red flags associated with ex-offenders.

As an ex-offender, you need to overcome these possible barriers to getting an interview and job offer. You can start by writing letters that avoid the many writing errors committed by ex-offenders and other job seekers. You need to present a picture of someone who is well organized, sincere, purposeful, willing and able to take responsibility, and who tells the truth. Most important of all, you need to clearly communicate that you **can add value to an employer's operations**.

Ex-Offender Letters to Avoid

We receive numerous letters from ex-offenders who request various forms of assistance – their goal in writing to us is to persuade. While some of the letters are painful yet touching to read, others appear to be obvious exercises in manipulation. Many letters from ex-offenders are filled with misspellings and grammatical errors, written on unattractive paper torn from spiral tablets, and include an obvious return address that shouts "prison inmate." They are handwritten, usually on both sides of the paper, and include scribbled corrections. In addition, many letters are disorganized, reflecting stream-of-consciousness thought processes, and lacking purpose. The writing is often negative and perspectives are unrealistic, indicating the individual lacks self-esteem and goals, and possibly lives in a fantasy world filled with illusions.

Most letters we receive from ex-offenders include many errors that would immediately knock them out of consideration had they been written for the purpose of finding a job. While some of these errors are a function of one's incarceration – lack of computer access, limited paper options, and a prison return address – other errors, such as misspellings, grammatical errors, and organization, are based on literacy and education. Many of these errors can be corrected by following certain rules of good letter writing.

Whatever you do, don't assume you are a good letter writer just because you wrote many letters while in prison. Remember, practice does not make perfect – **practice tends to make certain habits, including writing errors, permanent!** Accordingly, you may have lots to learn in the following pages as we focus on the art of good letter writing for finding a job.

The World of Job Search Letters

Few job seekers understand the important role of letters in conducting a successful job search. Preoccupied with writing their resume or focusing on applications, they frequently neglect other equally important writing activities. Most of these writing activities center on **key letters** that may or may not accompany a resume. The major types of job search letters include:

- Job search start-up letters
- Laying the groundwork letters
- Networking letters
- Resume letters
- Cover letters
- Vacancy announcement letters
- Thank-you letters
- Special and unusual letters

Some letters actually substitute for a resume, whereas other letters should accompany a resume. Examples of these different types of job search letters are presented in Chapters 8, 9, and 10 of this book.

Importance of Cover Letters

In this chapter we focus on one of the most important letters you will ever write – the cover letter. We'll address other type of job search letters in later chapters. As the name suggests, a cover letter provides **cover** for your resume. Expertly crafted in reference to the content of your resume and your major strengths, this letter can make a big difference in whether or not you will be invited to a job interview.

All too many job seekers spend days, if not weeks, writing their resume to be sure they have the "perfect" document. Then, not realizing how important the cover letter is, they simply "throw" it together at the last minute and send it out with the resume. What a poor and ineffective way to manage a job search! For years, professional resume writers have subscribed to the following beliefs:

- 33% of employers read the cover letter first
- 33% of employers read the resume first and then, if they're interested, read the cover letter
- 33% of employers **never** read a cover letter

Now, we're learning that employers are reading cover letters more intently and using those letters to make decisions about which candidates to interview and which to exclude. Many comment that **it's often the cover letter, rather than the resume, that clearly separates one candidate from another**. As such, your cover letter deserves the same amount of attention and hard work as your resume!

Cover Letter Basics

Before we can begin our discussion on cover letter writing, it is important to understand what a cover letter is, what its purpose is, and who needs one. So, let's begin with the basics:

Cover Letter: A brief document (usually one page) that highlights an individual's skills, qualifications, training, employment history, and/or special skills for a specific position or type of position. An effective cover letter will answer the all-important question every employer asks: "Why should I invite this person for an interview and perhaps hire him or her?"

Cover letters are most effective when you have a targeted position in mind. Consider this: when you write your resume, you're writing a document that you can, hopefully, use for any position you apply for. Your cover letter, on the other hand, should be customized each time that you write it, allowing you to highlight the **specific** skills and experience you have that are most related to a **specific** employer's needs.

Purpose of a Cover Letter: To get an employer to **take action** and invite you for an interview. As such, your entire cover letter should focus on persuading an employer that you have the skills, qualifications, training, and/or experience they are seeking for a particular position or for general employment opportunities.

Who Needs a Cover Letter: Everyone who sends a resume. No matter the type of job, the industry, or the salary range of the position, everyone needs a cover letter. All employers expect to receive a cover letter when you send your resume, and because you can customize your letters to each specific position, it is an extremely valuable tool for your job search.

Now that you have a basic understanding of what a cover letter is, its purpose, and who needs one, we'll take it one step further and explore:

- the 3 types of cover letters
- the 3 cover letter formats
- the top 10 things you must know about cover letters
- the top 10 cover letter writing mistakes to avoid
- the top 10 cover letter production and distribution mistakes to avoid

Read these sections carefully, for they include information that is essential to writing cover letters that open doors and help generate interviews.

Types of Cover Letters

There are three basic types of cover letters that you will most likely use during your job search. Although the content of these letters may be similar, the greatest distinctions between the three types are (1) the purpose of the letter and (2) how the letter begins. Carefully review the three following boxes which list each type of letter and its purpose, along with a sample introductory paragraph.

- **Ad Response Letters:** Letters written in response to specific advertisements in newspapers and from online job postings.

   Please accept this letter and resume in response to your advertisement for a Retail Sales Associate. I believe that my experience closely matches your qualifications. I would appreciate an opportunity to interview for this position.

- **Cold-Call Letters:** Letters written to companies to express your interest in employment opportunities.

   Safely operating, maintaining, and repairing industrial machinery are what I do best. Now, I'm looking for the opportunity to work with an established company that is committed to the same quality standards and in need of talented, conscientious employees. Aware of your strong reputation, I know that Ace is the right place for me and I have enclosed my resume for your review.

- **Referral Letters:** Letters written to a company because another individual referred you to that person and/or organization.

  John Spencer, a former co-worker of mine, recommended I contact you to explore opportunities with your firm. John said that you were always in the market for qualified drivers and, with 12 years of cross-country driving experience, I'm anxious to meet with you to discuss my background and your current hiring needs. My resume is enclosed for your review.

Refer to the next three pages for examples of each of these letter types.

Cover Letter
(ad response)

882 Forest Lane
Cleveland, OH 43210
March 1, 20____

P.O. Box 82
Cleveland, OH 43207

Here's my resume in response to your ad in today's *Cleveland Plain Dealer* for an Evening Dispatcher. I'm very familiar – four years experience – with all aspects of trucking, warehouse, and communication operations. I worked as a driver for two years, a stevedore for one year, and an assistant warehouse manager for one year. I am familiar with computerized dispatch operations, and I'm noted for working well with others in stressful settings.

I would appreciate more information on this position and your organization, as well as an opportunity to interview for this position. I will follow up with a phone call next week to learn more. You will find I have a pleasant telephone manner which is essential for a good dispatcher.

Sincerely,

Jack Diamond

Jack Diamond
diamondj@earthnet.com

Cover Letter
(cold call)

PORTER MACKEL
3891 Terrace Lawn
Jacksonville, FL 35817
319-721-3827
Email: mackelp@net2.com

October 3, 20___

Martin Shephard
SOUTHERN REALTY
8189 King Street
Jacksonville, FL 35819

Dear Mr. Shephard:

Whoever said you can't get rich quick never met someone who made their fortune in real estate. While I may not be rich now, I hope to be one day. And it will be made in real estate working with one of the top agencies.

If you are looking for an energetic performer who knows how to sell and sell and sell, then we should talk soon. In the meantime, I enclose a copy of my resume for your reference.

I will call your office on Thursday afternoon to see if your schedule would permit us to meet in the very near future. I would really like to learn more about your firm and how I might fit into your plans for the future.

Sincerely,

Porter Mackel

Porter Mackel
mackelp@aol.com

Cover Letter

(referral)

2984 Independent Road
Wichita, KS 58722
April 19, 20 ____

Mark Watson
TLN Maintenance Group
8193 Center Street
Wichita, KS 58721

Dear Mr. Watson:

Michael Thiel recommended that I send you a copy of my resume for
your reference. He said he thought you might have a vacancy for a
groundskeeper with your new apartment complex at Overland
West.

I have several years of experience in all phases of groundskeeping
with both large and small companies. I'm especially knowledgeable
about landscaping details and am familiar with a variety of equipment used in maintaining lawns and gardens. I have an excellent
record for maintaining machinery to the highest standards and work
well independently.

Since I've worked with Michael on previous jobs, he knows my work
well. I'm sure he could answer any questions you may have about
my qualifications. I also have photos of several jobs I completed as
an independent contractor, which I would be happy to share with
you.

I will call you on Tuesday to answer any questions you may have
about my work. Perhaps we could get together to discuss how I
might best meet your future needs.

Sincerely,

Gary Olson

Gary Olson
olsong@erols.com

Cover Letter Formats

Letters also have different format characteristics. Cover letters normally are composed using three basic types of formats:

- **Paragraph Format:** Best to use when you're "telling a story" about yourself, your career, and/or your experiences. The paragraph format is the most common format for any type of business letter, including cover letters. Here's an example:

  Throughout my six years in geriatric nursing, I have come to develop an appreciation for the unique challenges associated with caring for an elderly population. These patients require much more than just physical nursing care; they also require a sympathetic and caring attitude, which is essential in gaining their cooperation and instilling a sense of trust. That is where I have excelled.

- **Bullet Format:** Best to use when trying to bring attention to different groups of skills, experiences, and/or achievements. The bullet format lets you include a lot of information, yet keep it all to a minimum in terms of space. Here's a quick example:

  - *Nine years of experience working as an automotive mechanic.*
  - *Excellent skills in troubleshooting and diagnosing automotive malfunctions.*
  - *Certified by Ford Motor Company as a "Qualified Mechanic."*
  - *Completed training with Ford, Chrysler, and Honda.*

- **"T" Format:** Best to use when you want to respond with how your skills and experiences match each of the requirements in an advertisement. When preparing this letter, you'll type all of the employer requirements on the left side of the page, and you'll type all of your relevant skills, experiences, qualifications, and more on the right side of the page. Here's an example:

Your Requirements	*My Qualifications*
Proficiency with MS Word	Three years of full-time secretarial experience working with MS Word, Access, and PowerPoint.
Strong organizational skills	Three years' experience managing a large real estate office with 25 agents; handled all administrative work.

Refer to the following four pages for examples of each of the three types of cover letter formats.

Cover Letter
(paragraph format)

7813 Peoria Avenue
Chicago, IL 60030

July 23, 20 ___

Emily Southern
Atlas Auto Supply
153 West 19th Street
Chicago, IL 60033

Dear Ms. Southern:

Please accept the enclosed resume as my application in response to your ad in today's *Chicago Tribune* for a Parts Manager. You stated you needed an experienced manager who has worked with large equipment and who is familiar with ordering inventory and managing personnel.

I believe I have the necessary experience and skills to do this job well. During the past 10 years I have worked at all levels and in a variety of positions in the parts business. I began in receiving, moved on to manage a stockroom, took customer orders, and managed a parts warehouse with 11 employees. I'm experienced in operating computerized inventory systems. In my last job I decreased warehouse labor costs by 35% by installing a new inventory system.

I would appreciate the opportunity to interview for this position. Please expect a phone call from me on Thursday afternoon. I'll be calling for more information about the position as well as to answer any questions you may have about my candidacy.

Sincerely,

Terry Wilder

Terry Wilder
wildert@hotmail.com

Cover Letter
(bullet format)

---

731 Ocean Breeze Dr.
Miami, FL 31114
February 7, 20 ___

Terry Barton
KEY MANAGEMENT CO.
7820 Ocean Blvd., Suite 131
Miami, FL 31110

Dear Mr. Barton:

I read with interest your ad in today's *Miami Herald* for a Building Engineer to handle a 78-unit condo project. I believe I have the necessary experience to do an excellent job. In addition, I am willing to live on the premises.

I have nearly seven years of experience as a Building Engineer. My experience involved:

- working with all aspects of central heating plants
- diagnosing and resolving mechanical, electrical, and plumbing problems
- preparing equipment for inspections
- reporting monthly inspections to the condo association president and presenting an annual inspection report to association members

I pride myself on operating an effective preventive maintenance program which includes timely inspections and routine reporting procedures.

I would appreciate an opportunity to interview for this position. I'm especially interested in sharing with you a model preventive maintenance program I developed that enabled a condo association to save over $100,000 a year in unnecessary repairs.

I'll call your office next Monday to see if you have any questions concerning my candidacy. I look forward to meeting you and learning more about the position.

Sincerely,

Samuel Rittenstone

Samuel Rittenstone
rittenstone@mymail.com

Cover Letter
("T" Letter Format)

September 21, 20____

Jack Tillman
ACE Electrical Solutions
2781 Washington Avenue
Baltimore, MD 17233

Dear Mr. Tillman:

I'm responding to your ad that appears in today's *Baltimore Sun* for an Electrician.
I believe I am an excellent candidate for this position. I would bring to this
position the following qualifications:

Your Requirements	My Qualifications
One year commercial experience	Completed one-year apprentice-ship and served two years as an electrician's helper.
Responsible	Praised by previous employer as being a quick starter who takes initiative, is responsible, and gets the job done on time.
Trouble-shooter	Skilled in solving complex wiring problems that have saved customers additional costs.
Good customer relations	Received several letters from customers expressing satisfaction for quickly solving problems and saving money.

In addition, I know the importance of building strong long-term customer relations. I enjoy taking on new challenges and working with teams to achieve
company goals.

I believe there is a strong match between your needs and my qualifications. Could
we meet soon to discuss how we might best work together? I'll call your office on
Wednesday at 11am to see if your schedule might permit such a meeting.

Sincerely,

Aaron Easton

Aaron Easton
eastonar@hotmail.com

The Top 10 Things You Must Know About Cover Letters

Effective letter writers follow many of the following observations and principles of letter writing:

1. **There are few hard and fast rules for writing cover letters.** Similar to resumes, there are few rules for writing cover letters, what information to include, how to include it, and why. The only real guideline for cover letter writing is to create a document that "sells" you for the job you are pursuing by highlighting your most relevant skills, experiences, talents, and qualifications that are directly related to the position or types of position you are applying for.

    How you accomplish that is what this chapter and the next (cover letter samples) are all about. All of these letters are presented as tools for use in writing your own winning cover letters, so feel free to borrow wording and/or formatting that is right for you.

2. **One page is generally the best.** Unless your situation is most unusual, a one-page cover letter is our recommendation, particularly if it's accompanying a one-page resume. Cover letters do not need to be long and wordy. Rather, they should be short and to the point, highlighting just the skills, experiences, and qualifications you have that are most related to the particular position for which you are applying. In fact, it's ideal if a prospective employer is able to quickly scan your cover letter, capture the key points, and instantly know that you're a qualified candidate whom they definitely want to interview.

3. **Effective cover letters include eight key components.** Although there are no precise rules for how to write a cover letter, most business letters (cover letters included) consist of eight key components, as listed below. Use the sample Standard Letter Elements template on page 142 for reference as to where to position each of these components in your cover letter.

    1. Heading
    2. Date line
    3. Inside address
    4. Salutation or greeting
    5. Body of letter

6. Closing
7. Signature line
8. Enclosure line

1. HEADING

The heading for your cover letter should include your name, address, telephone number, cell phone number (if you have a cell phone), and email address (if you have one). You can present this information in one of two formats:

Letterhead Format:

JOHN JENNINGS

458 Craigmont Avenue   Home: (555) 932-3982
Smithtown, PA 19809   Email: jjenn@aol.com

Standard Business Letter Format:

212 E. Main Street
Duluth, MN 59098
(555) 382-3828

2. DATE LINE

The date line comes immediately after the heading and, generally, will be presented as month, day, and year: March 12, 2005. It is best to leave at least one blank line between your heading and the date line. For example:

212 E. Main Street
Duluth, MN 59098
(555) 382-3828

May 12, 2005

3. INSIDE ADDRESS

The inside address consists of the title, name, position, company, and address of the individual receiving your letter. The following rules should always be followed:

TITLE: Always address your letter recipient by his or her proper title:

Mr.	male
Mrs.	married female
Miss	unmarried female
Ms.	female if unsure of marital status
Dr.	doctor

NAME: Always try to address your letter to a specific person by name. Write the name in full – no nicknames, shortened forms, or abbreviations other than the middle initial.

POSITION: This is normally one's job title within an organization such as General Manager, Accounting Manager, Vice President of Sales, or President.

COMPANY: Complete name of the organization, including any subdivisions such as departments, sections, or offices.

ADDRESS: Street address or post office box, city, state and zip code. Here's an example:

Mr. Jeff Delancey
General Manager
Smith Industries, Inc.
321 E. Wood Boulevard
Chicago, IL 60689

4. SALUTATION OR GREETING

The salutation should consist of the greeting "Dear" followed by the proper title and surname of the individual. Unless you are a close friend, never address the individual by his or her first name. Such an informal greeting is inappropriate for job search letters. A colon – not a comma – always follows the individual's last name:

Dear Ms. Reynolds:

5. BODY OF LETTER

The body of your cover letter is, by far, the most important part of your letter. Within just a few short paragraphs or bulleted items you will highlight the skills, qualifications, and experience that you have which are most related to **that** company's specific needs. Be sure to keep your paragraphs short for easy reading; we recommend no more than five typed lines per paragraph. If you're using a bullet-style letter, be sure to keep the number of bullets to five or six. And, when writing your sentences, be sure to keep each sentence to 20 words or less. Longer sentences are confusing and often difficult to understand, so keep your sentences simple and to the point.

6. CLOSING

The closing of your cover letter can take many different forms. The most standard are:

> Sincerely,
> Sincerely yours,
> Cordially,
> Cordially yours,
> Respectfully,
> Respectfully yours,

7. SIGNATURE LINE

Your signature information should be on two lines. First, your typed name should appear four spaces below the closing, leaving enough room for you to put your handwritten signature into the blank space. We recommend that you sign your letters with a blue fountain pen or ballpoint pen for the most professional appearance.

> Sincerely,
>
> *Ronald R. Jensen*
>
> Ronald R. Jensen

8. ENCLOSURE LINE

Chances are that whenever you send a cover letter, you'll be sending it along with your resume. As such, be certain to write the word "Enclosure" at the very end of your cover letter, two lines down from where your signature line was typed.

Sincerely,

Ronald R. Jensen

Ronald R. Jensen

Enclosure

4. **Address your letter to a specific person.** Whenever possible – and that should be most of the time – address your cover letter to a specific person rather than a department or a company. If the name is not listed in an advertisement (send your resume to the Human Resources Director), call and get that individual's name. All business letters, cover letters included, are much better received when addressed to someone versus anyone. Furthermore, once you know the name of the individual you're sending your resume and cover letter to, you can then call to follow up, ask for that person by name, and address them by name. We guarantee they'll be impressed that you took the extra effort.

If, after your research, you are still unable to identify an individual's name, we recommend one of two methods to address your cover letter:

Address your letter to "Dear Sir/Madam," the formal, neutral, and most acceptable style.

OR

Eliminate the salutation ("Dear _____") entirely and start the letter with your opening paragraph. Remember the old saying, *"When in doubt, leave it out."*

Standard Letter Elements

(1) *heading*

(2) *date line*

(3) *inside address*

(4) *salutation*

(5) *body*

(6) *closing*

(7) *signature line*

(8) *enclosure*

5. **Do not handwrite your cover letter.** If you are used to handwriting your letters, it's now time to switch to typing. In decades past, when people still actually handwrote letters, business correspondence, reports, and more, it was important to have good penmanship. Now that virtually the entire world is computerized, handwriting is not as important a consideration, although it is still valued by many. As such, do not fall back on the "olden days" and handwrite your cover letters. It is not acceptable in today's modern workplace, no matter the type of job, company, or industry. You put your best professional effort forward when you neatly type your letters. Handwritten thank-you letters are often used by realtors, car salesmen, and insurance agents who believe they need a "personal touch" to close a sale. Finding a job is not the same as selling real estate, cars, and insurance! However, if you are still incarcerated and do not have access to a computer, go ahead and handwrite your letters if you have no other options, but make sure they are written neatly and on good quality paper. Try to project as professional an image as possible given your production limitations.

6. **Be assertive in your follow-up.** It only takes seven simple words to kill your cover letter and deaden your job search:

    I look forward to hearing from you.

    Even five words will do it: *"Thank you for your consideration."* These typical cover letter closings are what we refer to as passive closings. In essence, you're putting the responsibility for follow-up in the hands of the recipient of your letter, and that approach is wrong.

    To be an effective job seeker, you want to be assertive and take control of your own job search and your own destiny. As such, you want to close your cover letters with a sentence or two that details how you plan to follow up and what specific action you plan to take.

    Here are a few follow-up statements that you might consider for your cover letters:

    > *I will call your office next Thursday morning, September 12, to see if your schedule would permit us to meet briefly. Thank you for your consideration.*

    > *I will call your office next Tuesday afternoon at 2:30pm to ask you a few questions and see when we might schedule a personal interview. Thank you.*

> *Would next week be a good time to discuss my interest in the position? I'll call your office at 11 am on Wednesday to check your schedule. Thank you and I appreciate your time.*

By taking action after mailing a cover letter, you're demonstrating three very important characteristics that every company values: (1) your initiative, (2) your interest in the position, and (3) your interest in the company.

7. **100% accuracy and perfection are critical standards for cover letters.** Forbidden: typographical, spelling, punctuation, and grammatical errors. Your letter reflects the quality of work that you will produce for a company, so be sure that it's perfect. Nothing less is acceptable.

   When you have finished writing your letter, have two or three people proofread it to be sure that you haven't missed anything or made any mistakes. Even though you might proofread it 10 times yourself, it is always better to have another pair of eyes review the letter, just to double-check that it is indeed perfect. The cover letter that you submit to a company today is your one and only chance to make an excellent first impression. Don't let a ridiculous typographical error stand in your way!

8. **Do not include salary information in your letter.** The purpose of your cover letter is to interest a company in your background, experience, and skills. It is not the place to discuss salary history (what you've earned in the past) or salary requirements (what you want to make now). In fact, research has shown that even when a company asks for salary information in an advertisement, if they are impressed with your qualifications and you have not included that information in your letter, they will still contact you for an interview!

   As explained in Chapter 1, the time and place to discuss salary is during an interview, once you have had the chance to learn more about the position and the company, and once the company has had the chance to meet and get to know you. Then, and only then, is it time to discuss your salary. For expert advice on salary negotiations, specifically for ex-offenders, please refer to *The Ex-Offender's Job Hunting Guide* (Impact Publications, 2005).

9. **Do not include references in your cover letter.** Here's how the job search process works. First, an employer reviews your resume and letter, and then, if they are impressed with your skills and experience, they will contact you

to schedule an interview. Once you've proceeded successfully through the interview (or, perhaps, several rounds of interviews) and the company is considering making you an offer of employment, then, and only then, will it be necessary to provide your list of references. When someone is reviewing your resume and cover letter for the first time, they will not be interested in your references until they have met and interviewed you. Only then, after they are impressed with you, will they be willing to take the time to check out your references to find out what they have to say about you.

10. **Do not disclose your prison record in your cover letter.** As we explained in Chapter 1, the time and place to discuss your incarceration is during the actual job interview, after you've had the chance to meet your interviewer and impress him or her with your qualifications. At that point, your prison record will become something important to discuss, but not a reason to not interview you. Never include any negative information in your cover letter, or you'll instantly give the prospective employer a reason to exclude you from consideration.

The Top 10 Cover Letter Writing Mistakes to Avoid

In the preceding pages, we've outlined the top 10 things that every job seeker must know about writing cover letters. Now, we're going to switch gears and focus on the top 10 cover letter writing mistakes that you must avoid in order to move your job search forward in an effective and positive manner.

All too often job seekers submit cover letters with serious writing errors, errors that we can almost guarantee will put you out of the running for a job. A prospective employer will think to himself, "If this is the quality of work that this individual produces, I certainly don't want them in my organization. I can't have the company sending out work that is confusing and disorganized, with typographical, grammatical, and wording errors!"

To be sure that this doesn't happen to you, avoid the following common errors:

1. Letter does not highlight why you're qualified for the advertised position.
2. Letter is too long or too short.
3. Letter is unattractive and uses a typestyle that is too small, making it extremely difficult to read.

4. Letter does not include contact information, such as telephone number, mailing address, and email address.
5. Letter is sloppy with handwritten corrections.
6. Letter has misspellings, poor grammar, and punctuation errors.
7. Letter is wordy and repetitive.
8. Letter includes information that seems suspicious and untruthful.
9. Resume lacks credibility and content and includes lots of fluff and canned cover letter language.
10. Resume uses jargon and abbreviations unknown to the reader.

Top 10 Cover Letter Production and Distribution Mistakes to Avoid

After you have written your cover letter and carefully reviewed it to be sure that you haven't committed any of the 10 critical letter writing mistakes, it's time to move on to the actual typing and distribution of your cover letter. Again, there are common errors that you can easily avoid if you pay close attention to detail. Here's what you should avoid:

1. Letter is poorly typed, making it difficult to read.
2. Letter is printed on odd-sized, poor-quality, or extremely thin or thick paper.
3. Letter is soiled with coffee stains, fingerprints, ink marks, or even lipstick smears.
4. Resume is mailed, faxed, or emailed to "To Whom It May Concern" or "Dear Sir." (Be smart ... call and get a name whenever possible!)
5. Letter is mailed in a tiny envelope that requires it to be unfolded and flattened several times.
6. Letter is mailed in an envelope that is double-sealed with tape and virtually impossible to open.
7. Back of envelope includes a handwritten note stating that something is missing in the letter, that the phone number has changed, or some other important message.
8. Letter arrives without proper postage, and the company has to pay!
9. Letter repeats exactly what's on the resume, is not interesting, and does not encourage the reader to take action (call you for an interview).
10. Letter has typographical, grammatical, wording, and/or punctuation errors.

Sample Cover Letters

FOLLOWING ARE FOUR SAMPLE cover letters that you can use to get ideas for how to write and design your own letters. These are actual cover letters used by ex-offenders from prisons throughout the United States, although the names, addresses, phone numbers, and other personal information has been changed to protect each person's privacy. Each cover letter is presented with the resume that it accompanied so that you can see how each resume and cover letter package worked together to create just the "right" image of the job search candidate.

Here's how you can best use these cover letters:

- Copy letter designs that you like.
- Borrow words that are appropriate for your skills and experience.
- Use similar formats and typestyles.
- Get ideas for how to highlight the most important things about your background and qualifications.
- Learn how to draw special attention to important achievements and contributions.
- Identify ways to overcome potential hiring objections.

To understand why these cover letters were written and designed the way that they were, read the following information about each one as you review it.

Letter:	**Jason P. Baso**, page 150-152
Prison:	1997 to 2005
Writer:	Gina Taylor, Gina Taylor & Associates
Objective:	Position as a Heavy Equipment Operator, Driver, or Laborer
Strategy:	Letter written in response to an advertisement for a Heavy Equipment Operator. Bullet-style letter used to highlight most relevant qualifications from work experience and educational background. Final two short paragraphs summarize additional related skills and communicate how the job seeker will follow up to arrange an interview.

Letter:	**Roy F. Zackary**, page 153-154
Prison:	2003 to 2005
Writer:	Andrea Howard, NYS Department of Labor
Objective:	Position as an Automotive Mechanic
Strategy:	Letter written at the recommendation of a friend who suggested the job seeker use his name to help open doors and generate interview. Short letter highlights (1) why this individual recommended him, (2) his core skills as they relate to the position, and (3) a closing paragraph that explains how he'll follow up to schedule an interview.

Letter:	**James O'Brien**, page 155-157
Prison:	2003
Writer:	Bob Simmons, Career Transition Associates
Objective:	Position as a Training and Development Professional
Strategy:	Cold-call letter written to uncover relevant professional opportunities that may exist with major corporations in the job seeker's geographic area. Short and concise style that clearly illustrates professional skills, personal talents, and notable educational credentials. Assertive closing states that job seeker will follow up to schedule an interview.

Letter:	**Jack Smith**, page 158-160
Prison:	1997 to 2005

Writer: Bill Murdock, The Employment Coach

Objective: Position in Sales and/or Operations Manager in the boating industry

Strategy: Cold-call letter used to uncover sales opportunities within the targeted industry. Unique combination paragraph/bullet style draws immediate visual attention to his abilities in sales, management, and business, and follows with specific achievements that relate to each of his three core skill areas. Open-ended closing allows job seeker or company to follow up to schedule the interview.

JASON P. BASO

1234 Campbell   -   Kansas City, Missouri 64108
(816) 123-4567

October 12, 20___

Ms. Eileen Markham
Vice President of Construction Operations
Ryland Homes, Inc.
777 East Hanover Street
Kansas City, MO 64132

Dear Ms. Markham:

I am writing in response to your advertisement for a Heavy Equipment Operator and have enclosed my resume for your review. Highlights of my experience that may be of interest to you include:

- Hands-on experience operating forklifts, tractors, loaders, backhoes, motor graders, track loaders, bulldozers, bobcat skid/steer loaders, and scrapers.

- Attended Certified Heavy Equipment Operator course at Linn State Technical College.

- Completion of several Computer Information Systems courses to further my career.

My work-related skills are solid. I can read and interpret technical documents, drawings, maintenance manuals, repair instructions, and more. In addition, I have clearly demonstrated my ability to work independently, productively, and efficiently.

To have the opportunity to work for Ryland Homes would be a great opportunity and I am most interested in meeting with you as soon as your schedule allows. I will call Tuesday morning, October 17th so that we can coordinate a specific date and time for an interview. Thank you for your time and your consideration. I guarantee it will be worth it.

Sincerely,

Jason P. Baso

Enclosure

JASON P. BASO

1234 Campbell - Kansas City, Missouri 64108
(816) 123-4567

AREAS OF RELEVANT SKILLS

Multi-dimensional individual with experience as a **heavy equipment operator, driver,** and **laborer**. Technical knowledge in surveying, welding, and general maintenance. Excellent safety record and willing to do more than what is expected. Communicate and interact effectively with diverse cultures.

- ❖ **Heavy Equipment**: Forklift, Tractor, Loader, Backhoe, Motor Grader, Track Loader, Bulldozer, Bobcat Skid/Steer Loader, Scraper
- ❖ **Driver**: Dump Truck, Over-the-Road
- ❖ **Technical**: Surveying, Welding
- ❖ **Maintenance**: General, Preventive, Carpentry, Painting

EDUCATIONAL BACKGROUND

Northwest Missouri Community College   Jefferson City, MO
    Introduction to Computer Information Systems; Basic Programming
    Data Files; Structural Programming; Microcomputer Operating Systems

Linn State Technical College   Linn, MO
    Heavy Equipment Operator Certificate Course
    Welding; Blue Print Interpretation; Surveying; Preventive Maintenance

American Truck Driving School   Waco, TX
    Over-The-Road Truck Driving Certificate Course

EMPLOYMENT HISTORY

TEMPORARY ASSIGNMENTS, Jefferson City & Cameron, MO   1997 - 2005
- ➤ Store Clerk/Stocker
- ➤ Library Clerk/Data Entry Clerk
- ➤ Computer Operator/Data Entry Clerk
- ➤ Chapel Head Clerk
- ➤ AM/PM Baker/Store Clerk

LINN TECHNICAL COLLEGE, Linn, MO   1996
MAINTENANCE TECHNICIAN
General maintenance, cleaning, carpentry, and lawn care.

SPRINGFIELD RECREATION DEPARTMENT, Springfield, MO   1995
LABORER, Park Maintenance

JASON P. BASO

RESUME, Page 2

EMPLOYMENT HISTORY
(Continued)

MAZZIO'S PIZZA, Springfield, MO   1994 - 1995
  DELIVERY DRIVER

TEMPORARY ASSIGNMENTS, Springfield, MO & Maumee, OH   1992 - 1994
  - Roofer
  - Fork-lift Operator
  - Delivery Driver
  - Painter

NORTH AMERICAN VAN LINES, Ft. Wayne, IN   1990 - 1992
  OVER-THE-ROAD DRIVER

Roy F. Zackary

423 Clover Ave ~ Apt. 12F   518.689.2736   Albany, NY 12210

June 15, 20___

Mr. Peter Sandrine
Century Automotive
2397 Broyhill Road
West Clarksville, NY 12077

RE: **Auto Mechanic Career Opportunity**

Dear Mr. Sandrine,

Upon a recommendation from Jon Whyle, I am submitting my resume for the auto mechanic position that you seek to fill. Having worked for you as the Assistant Sales Manager for over two years, Mr. Whyle has the benefit of understanding your staffing needs. He speaks highly of your operation and feels as though my mechanical background would greatly benefit Century Automotive.

I would come to you with a multitude of mechanical and trade-related abilities, in addition to proven success resolving customer concerns. With customer satisfaction being at the forefront of repeat business, technicians who can make customers feel respected are a rare commodity.

I will call you next week to discuss my resume and qualifications in greater detail. Should you wish to contact me sooner, I can be reached at 518.689.2736.

Respectfully,

Roy F. Zackary

Roy F. Zackary

Enclosure

ROY F. ZACKARY

423 Hillview Ave ~ Apt. 3-B   518.223.2743   Albany, NY 12210

AUTOMOBILE MECHANIC / DETAILER

Highly motivated with a genuine desire to succeed. Outstanding employability reviews and professional recommendations highlighting positive attitude in addition to above average technical skills.

Over six years combined experience working in the skilled trades; mechanics, automotive detailing, and building maintenance. Graduate of NYS-accredited training programs.

Additional skills include customer relations, inventory, and personnel management.

Possess a clean class "D" NYS driver's license.

Employability Skills

Automotive Mechanics and Detailing

- Diagnosed and repaired mechanical defects through diagnostic testing, engine sounds, and visual observations of parts. Estimated labor and material requirements.
- Rebuilt break, ignition, and carburetor systems, overhauled transmissions and differentials, and recommended preventative maintenance in accordance with manufacturer recommendations (e.g., tire rotation and balance, oil change and fluid checks, tune up, brake and belt replacement).
- Detailed vehicles for sale.

Business / Personnel Management

- Oversaw financial details (e.g., payroll, bank deposits, bookkeeping).
- Worked closely with wholesalers in order to maintain appropriate inventory.
- Trained and supervised employees on cash register operation and customer relations.

Building / Custodial Maintenance

- Carpentry - Hung sheetrock, framed, hung cabinets, and installed replacement windows.
- Painting – Primed and painted interiors and exteriors.
- Plumbing – Repaired and rebuilt piping systems to eliminate leaks and reduce damage.

Education

Clinton Auto Mechanic Technical ~ Dannemora, NY
- Mechanics Certificate of Completion ~ 9/2002

Albany High School ~ Albany, NY
- Diploma ~ Building Maintenance Concentration ~ 1997

Employment History

Automobile Mechanic ~ 2002 – 2005
    New York State Department of Corrections ~ Dannemora, NY
    Marshall's Hyundai ~ Albany, NY

Auto Detailer ~ 2000 - 2002
    Central Car Wash ~ Albany NY

Assistant Manager ~ 1999 - 2000
    Subway ~ Glens Falls, NY

JAMES O'BRIEN

64 Lincoln Avenue
Holtsville, New York 11742
Home: 631-582-4320; Cell: 516 562-1857
E-Mail: JamesOb26@optonline.net

December 10, 20____

Mr. Josh Greene
The Allian Corporation
321 E. Walnut Street
Pittsburgh, PA 19837

Dear Mr. Greene:

You may have a need for a highly energetic, articulate, and dedicated Training and Development professional. If so, I am just the candidate you've been searching for.

My career in teaching has illustrated excellent platform abilities in motivating participants no matter what the size of the population. Evaluations of my performance have acknowledged my abilities in identifying and adapting my presentations to the needs of the participants.

I have also excelled in training and motivating participants on an individual basis.

The enclosed resume further illustrates my talents and accomplishments.

I am well-educated, possessing two Masters Degrees.

I would welcome the opportunity to discuss with you at your convenience how I might join your organization and enhance your Training and Development efforts. I'll follow up with your next Thursday to see when an appointment interview time would be. Thank you.

Sincerely,

James O'Brien

James O'Brien

Enclosure

JAMES O'BRIEN
64 Lincoln Avenue
Holtsville, New York 11742
Home: 631-582-4320; Cell: 516 562-1857
E-Mail: JamesOb26@optonline.net

OBJECTIVE

Training and Development Opportunity

SUMMARY

A highly motivated and skilled Training and Development professional. Demonstrated capabilities include designing and implementing programs, adapting presentations to participant needs, and ensuring follow-up goals are achieved. Excel in performance in both group and individual settings. Background is enhanced by fluency in Spanish. A resourceful, adaptable, and dedicated self-starter who is detail oriented and possesses excellent communication abilities.

Computer proficiency includes MS Word, PowerPoint, Excel, Access, Publisher, and Outlook.

SELECTED ACCOMPLISHMENTS AND RESPONSIBILITIES

- Researched, designed, and implemented curricula covering varied and diverse populations.

- Modified and adapted existing curricula to adhere to state mandates. Consistently achieved goals.

- Developed and instituted follow-up methods to ensure program objectives were met.

- Conducted presentations for up to 200 participants.

- Successfully communicated with students in addressing both their everyday and personal concerns.

- Prepared weekly presentations covering different subjects.

- Designed and implemented participant activities which stimulated learning and required the use of computer technology.

- Trained newly hired staff by conducting workshops and mentoring several new educators.

- Motivated students and staff by developing and implementing a program which recognized academic achievements and excellence for both students and staff members.

JAMES O'BRIEN Cell Phone: 516-562-1857 **Page 2**

SELECTED ACCOMPLISHMENTS AND RESPONSIBILITIES (Continued)

- Served on numerous project planning committees which successfully addressed ongoing concerns of daily operations, identified problems, and provided solutions.

- Chaired policy review board that provided and promoted staff development programs.

- Participated in developing and instituting a technology plan for the school building and language department personnel.

- Developed and presented several academic workshops using PowerPoint for participants at the national, regional, and local levels.

PROFESSIONAL EXPERIENCE

LINCOLN CENTRAL SCHOOL DISTRICT, Riverhead, NY (1986 – 2002)
Spanish Teacher

Additional Experience: Temporary positions in the hospitality, retail, and food service industries (2003 – Present)

EDUCATION

HUNTER COLLEGE, New York, NY (1998)
Master of Science Degree, School Administration and Supervision
Certificate of Staff Development

STATE UNIVERSITY OF NEW YORK, Albany, NY (1994)
Master of Arts Degree, Liberal Studies in Education

SOUTHAMPTON COLLEGE, Southampton, NY (1986)
Bachelor of Arts Degree, Romance Languages

PROFESSIONAL AFFILIATION

American Society for Training and Development (ASTD)

FOREIGN LANGUAGE

Fluent in Spanish

JACK SMITH

July 15, 20____
5712 Roosevelt Way
Seattle, Washington 989910
725.465.7700
Jsmith2005@aol.com

Dear Sir/Madam:

I'm seeking a new opportunity in boat sales and, with extensive experience in both sales and management, including luxury yachts, I believe I bring quite a bit to the table. My resume is enclosed.

Most recently, I have been spurring sales growth for Puget Sound Boating and it's gone quite well – a 50% increase in revenues and profits within 60 days. Prior to that, as the General Sales and Operations Manager for Snohomish Yachts , I correctly anticipated that new yacht sales would hit the tank in 2000 and repositioned the sales effort toward used consignment products. Today, this decision has resulted in 90% of their sales, plus contributes significant monthly slip rentals.

As I consider how to best introduce myself to you, three themes emerge very quickly:

- **I can sell.**

  For sixteen years, I ranked in the "Top Five" of all Life Insurance of America salespersons, and most recently with Bothell Marine, I was nationally ranked with each line the dealership carried, at times personally outselling entire dealerships.

- **I can manage effectively.**

  As the owner of JS & S Investments, a specialized physician-based insurance agency, I oversaw operations in eight markets and four states. I am well versed in all aspects of daily operations.

- **I understand business.**

  Perhaps my strongest asset is my proven ability to identify and maximize an opportunity. Starting with my role as a nationally ranked life insurance salesperson, to my business ownership, and then with my experiences with P & L responsibility for retail luxury product sales, my success has been grounded in my in-depth feel for what business is all about.

As you can see, the combination of sales ability and business management experiences gives me quite a bit to talk about. I look forward to meeting with you in person to discuss how I can add value to your organization and drive sales and revenues straight to the bottom line.

Sincerely,

Jack Smith

Jack Smith
Enclosure

JACK SMITH

5712 Roosevelt Way
Seattle, Washington 98991
725.465.7700
Jsmith2005@aol.com

GENERAL SALES AND OPERATIONS MANAGER
Luxury Products / Financial Planning / Multi-Unit Operations

An exceptionally skilled sales professional with an unbroken record of consistent nationally ranked performance. Hands-on executive and managerial experience ranging from multi-unit / multi-state operations to developing industry-specific account penetration strategies.

Bachelor of Science – Psychology (1996)
CENTRAL WASHINGTON UNIVERSITY – Ellensburg, Washington
Significant Coursework toward a Bachelor of Business Administration Degree

PROFESSIONAL HIGHLIGHTS

Puget Sound Boating – Seattle, Washington
2004 to Present
General Manager / Sales Manager

Recruited to spur sales volumes and increase profitability for Seattle's largest boat dealership featuring eight lines of boats ranging from $15,000 to $65,000 (Monterey, Stingray, Voyager, Nautique, and Centurion among many) plus an additional six lines of trailers and fifth wheels.

- Drove sales from 40 units, and $800,000 in monthly revenues, to 60 units and, $1.3 million, within 60 days, by instituting formal selling processes and procedures. This represented a $700,000 increase over June and July YTD.
- Upgraded the finance department's capabilities. Trained a new F&I Manager and re-evaluated lending capabilities.
- Created the first documentation process for the company to chart both unit sales and revenues and allow YTD comparisons.
- Supervised the Make Ready, Service, Finance, and Sales departments. Approved commissions and payroll, resolved customer service issues, and consulted with vendors as necessary.

Snohomish Yachts – Seattle, Washington
2000 to 2003
Sales / Operations Manager

Profit and loss responsibility for both sales and operations for a full-service marina dealership featuring Doral Cruisers, Sugar Sand Jet Boards, and Destination Houseboats across a broad range of price points – $20,000 to $700,000.

- Implemented a consignment sales operation to offset revenue losses in new yacht sales. By 2003, realized 90% of sales through consignment brokerage fees with companion revenues of $9,000 in monthly moorage fees.
- Created marketing programs ranging from a quarterly direct mail newsletter (4,000 copies), newspaper, periodical, billboard, and radio advertising to trade show attendance. Approved content and presentation for the company's first website.
- Executed all administrative functions including daily sales and financial reports, vehicle titling, sales tax allocations, and insurance processing.

JACK SMITH

5712 Roosevelt Way
Seattle, Washington 98991
725.465.7700
Jsmith2005@aol.com

Bothell Marine – Bothell, Washington
1996 to 2000
Sales Manager - Yachts

Spearheaded the introduction of Cruiser, Chaparral, and Maxum Yacht lines to the Metroplex, achieving a peak of 57 unit sales and $6.5 million in revenues by 1998. Sustained market share against mainline competitors through 2000, with product price points from $120,000 to $400,000.

- Ranked fifth nationally within each line (Cruiser, Chaparral, Maxum) out of nearly 100 salespersons per line; personally accountable for sales volumes in excess of many dealerships.
- Created advertising strategies and marketing plans encompassing newspaper advertising, specialty presses, and trade (boat) shows.
- Negotiated for profitability, maintained inventory, and oversaw sales administration.

JS & S Financial – Portland, Oregon
1984 to 1991
Owner

Launched an insurance products-based financial planning company with an expanded, multi-line portfolio of investment products targeting physician and physician groups. Grew from a sole proprietorship to eight markets in Texas, the Carolina's, and the eastern seaboard producing over $3 million in annual premium.

- Negotiated program endorsements from state or municipal medical societies, paving the way for ongoing sales campaigns to physicians and other medical professionals.
- Sourced highly competitive executive life insurance policies and annuities for use in retirement planning.
- Oversaw policy administration, daily operations, and marketing for all eight satellite operations.

Life Insurance of America – Miami, Florida
1966 to 1984
Sales

A pioneering role advancing the concept of integrated life insurance programs as an integral part of sound financial planning. Targeted relocating executives from NASA, IBM, and Sears, providing financial strategies, identifying tax advantages, and offering competitive investment products from life insurance to annuities.

Championed the use of professional (medical) incorporation to sidestep stringent KEOGH contribution limitations. Ongoing recognition as one of the top life products representatives in the nation.

- Ranked number one in the nation in 1974, 1977, and 1978 for annual sales; continually recognized as one of the Top Five annual producers from a sales force of 850.
- First Life Insurance of America agent to individually eclipse $300,000 in annual premium.
- Guided the efforts of an eight-person administrative support staff in policy management, issuance, and documentation.

9

Writing Powerful Thank-You Letters

WHEN WAS THE LAST TIME you **received** a thank-you letter for something useful you did for someone or for an act of kindness you expressed? How did it make you feel toward that person? When was the last time you **wrote** a thank-you letter expressing your gratitude for someone else's assistance or act of kindness toward you? How do you think that letter made the other person feel about you?

Have you thought of writing a simple thank-you letter to a member of your family, a loved one, a teacher, a minister, a former employer, your lawyer, judge, warden, probation officer, or a complete stranger who gave you an important idea or new perspective – individuals who might be important in developing your network for finding a job? Have you ever thought of repairing damaged relationships, such as writing to a former employer who fired you or someone you hurt, by writing a thank-you letter? If not, this may be a good time to start "thinking outside the box" and begin repairing and developing better relationships in your job search network.

If you are not used to receiving or writing thank-you letters, you probably don't fully understand the power of such letters. People who receive these letters are usually **impressed** with the thoughtfulness of the writer and **remember**, in a positive manner, that person for what he or she did or said. People who write such letters often gain easy access, cooperation, and/or assistance from those who receive these letters. Best of all, when written after a job interview, thank-you letters often result in a job offer and a positive transition to a new job.

The Power of Thoughtfulness

Some of the most powerful letters you will ever write are thank-you letters. Much neglected by job seekers, these letters can make the difference in your job search. While these letters should be sent each and every time that you've had a job interview, they should also be sent during other important phases of your job search. Indeed, knowing when and how to write these letters may be more important than all your other job search activities.

It's important to understand what a thank-you letter is, what its purpose is, and who needs one. So, let's begin with the basics:

Thank-You Letter: A brief document, usually consisting of one page, although two pages are acceptable if there is a great deal of information that you want to communicate. When written following a job interview, your thank-you letter can accomplish four very important things:

1. Your thank-you letter gives you the opportunity to restate your interest in the position and the company.

2. Your thank-you letter demonstrates to your prospective employer that you follow through with things that you've started.

3. Your thank-you letter allows you to highlight important skills, qualifications, and experiences you may have forgotten to mention during the interview. Or, if you did mention those skills, you can restate them to be sure the company is aware of those specific qualifications that are essential for the job you've interviewed for.

4. Your thank-you letter lets you respond to any objections that may have been raised during the interview (for example, your prison record, your lack of experience with a particular type of equipment or computer program, the fact that you haven't worked for an extended period of time).

Purpose of a Thank-You Letter: To express your social graces and get someone to take action. If that someone is an employer, the primary purpose of the thank-letter is to either (1) invite you for a second interview or (2) offer you a job. (Be sure to send a different thank-you letter after your second interview and any others that may follow.)

> **Who Needs a Thank-You Letter:** Everyone needs to write thank-you letters throughout their job search but especially after each and every interview. The only exception to the rule would be if you were offered a job at the end of the first interview. In today's employment market, that is a relatively rare event, but it can happen. If so, congratulations!

Get Remembered As Thoughtful

Let's look at the variety of thank-you letters you should consider writing throughout your job search before we turn to specific examples of these letters.

Thank-you letters are some of the most effective communications in a job search. They demonstrate an important social grace that says something about you as an individual – your personality and how you probably relate to others. They communicate one of the most important characteristics sought in potential employees – thoughtfulness.

Better still, since few individuals write thank-you letters, those who write them are remembered by people who receive them. And one thing you definitely want to happen again and again during your job search is to be remembered by individuals who can provide you with useful information, advice, and referrals as well as invite you to job interviews and extend job offers. Being remembered as a thoughtful person with the proper social graces will give you an edge over job seekers who fail to write thank-you letters. Whatever you do, make sure you regularly send thank-you letters to individuals who assist you in your job search.

Many job seekers discover the most important letters they ever write are thank-you letters. These letters can have several positive outcomes:

- **Contacts turn into more contacts and job interviews:** A job seeker sends a thank-you letter to someone who recommended they contact a former classmate; impressed with the thoughtfulness of the job seeker and feeling somewhat responsible for helping him make the right contacts, the individual continues providing additional referrals, which eventually lead to two job interviews.

- **Job interview turns into a job offer:** A job seeker completes a job interview. Within 24 hours he writes a nice thank-you in which he expresses his gratitude for having an opportunity to interview for the position as well as restates his interest in working for the employer. This individual is then offered the job. The employer later tells him it was his thoughtful thank-you letter that gave him the edge over two other equally qualified candidates who never bothered to follow up after the interview.

- **A job rejection later turns into a job offer:** After interviewing for a position, a job seeker receives a standard rejection letter from an employer indicating the job was offered to another individual. Rather than get angry and end communications with the employer, the job seeker sends a nice thank-you letter in which he notes his disappointment in not being selected, yet thanks the interviewer for the opportunity. He also indicates his continuing interest in working for the organization. The employer remembers this individual. Rather than let him get away, he decides to create a new position for him.

- **A job offer turns into an immediate positive relationship:** After receiving a job offer, the new employee sends a nice thank-you letter expressing his enthusiasm in joining the company as well as stressing his appreciation for the confidence expressed in him by the employer. He also reassures the employer that he will be as productive as expected. This letter is well received by the employer, who is looking forward to working closely with such a thoughtful new employee. Indeed, he becomes a mentor and sponsor who immediately gives the employee some plum assignments that help him fast-track his career within the organization.

- **Resignation results in strong recommendations and a future job offer:** An employee, seeking to advance his career with a larger organization, receives a job offer from a competing firm. In submitting his formal letter of resignation, he also sends a personal thank-you letter to his former employer. He sincerely expresses his gratitude for having the opportunity to work with him and attributes much of his success to his mentoring. This letter further confirms the employer's conclusion about this former employee – he's losing a valuable asset. While he cannot offer him a similar or better career opportunity in this organization, he will keep him in mind if things change.

And things do change two years later when he makes a major career move to a much larger organization. One of the first things he does as Vice President is to begin shaping his own personal staff. He immediately contacts his past employee to see if he would be interested in working with him. He's interested and soon joins his former employer in making another major career move.

In these cases it was the job seekers' thank-you letters, rather than their cover letters and resumes, that got them job interviews and offers.

As indicated in the above cases, thank-you letters should be written in the following situations:

- **After receiving information, advice, or a referral from a contact:** You should always express your gratitude in writing to individuals who provide you with job search assistance. Not only is this a nice thing to do, it also contributes to a successful job search. Individuals who feel they are appreciated will most likely remember you and be willing to further assist you with your job search and recommend you to others.

- **Immediately after interviewing for a job:** Whether it be a telephone or face-to-face interview, always write a nice thank-you letter within 12 hours of completing the interview. This letter should express your gratitude for having an opportunity to interview for the job. Be sure to restate your interest in the job and stress your possible contributions to the employer's operations. The letter should emphasize your major strengths in relationship to the employer's needs. All other things being equal, this letter may give you an extra edge over other candidates. It may well prove to be your most effective letter in your entire job search!

- **Withdrawing from further consideration:** At some point during the recruitment process, you may decide to withdraw from further consideration. Perhaps you decided to take another job, you're now more satisfied with your present job, or the position no longer interests you. For whatever reason, you should write a short thank-you letter in which you withdraw from consideration. Explain in positive terms why you are no longer interested in pursuing an application with the organization, and thank them for their time and consideration.

- **After receiving a rejection:** Even if you receive a rejection, it's a good idea to write a thank-you letter. How many employers ever receive such a letter from what is probably a disappointed job seeker? This unique letter is likely to be remembered – which is what you want to accomplish in this situation. Being remembered may result in referrals to other employers or perhaps a job interview and offer at some later date.

- **After receiving a job offer:** However well they think they hire, employers still are uncertain about the outcome of their hiring decisions until new employees perform in their organization. Why not put their initial anxieties at ease and get off on the right foot by writing a nice thank-you letter? In this letter express your appreciation for having received the confidence and trust of the employer. Repeat what you told the employer during the job interview(s) about your goals and expected performance. Conclude with statements of your starting date and how much you look forward to becoming a productive member of the team. Such a thoughtful letter will be well received by the employer and could help you advance with the company.

- **Upon leaving a job:** Whether you leave your job voluntarily or are forced by circumstances to terminate, try to leave a positive part of you behind by writing a thank-you letter. Burning bridges behind you through face-to-face confrontation or a vindictive, get-even letter may later catch up with you, especially if you anger someone in the process who may later be in a position to affect your career. Remember, most people live in a small world where they often cross paths with people they've worked with before. If you quit to take a job with another organization, thank your employer for the time you spent with the organization and the opportunities given to you to acquire valuable experience and skills. If you terminated under difficult circumstances – organizational cutbacks or a nasty firing – try to leave on as positive a note as possible. Employers in such situations would rather have you out of sight and mind. Assure them there are no hard feelings, and you wish them the best as you would hope they would wish you the same. Stress the positives of your relationship with both the employer and the organization.

Remember, your future employer may call your previous employer for information on your past performance. If you leave a stressful situation on a positive note, chances are your previous employer will give you the benefit of the doubt and stress only your positives to others. He may even commit a few "sins of omission" that only you and he know about: "He really worked well with his co-workers and was one of our best clerks" does not tell the whole story, which may be that you couldn't get along with your boss and vice versa. After having made peace with each other with a thank-you letter, what would your former employer have to gain by telling the whole story to others about your work with him? Your thank-you letter should at least neutralize the situation and at best turn a negative situation into a positive for your career. Indeed, he may well become one of your supporters – for other jobs with other employers, that is!

Examples of each type of letter, written according to our principles of effective thank-you letters, appear at the end of this chapter and are identified accordingly.

Timely Writing

Thank-you letters should always be written in a timely manner. Make it a practice to sit down and write these letters within 12 hours of the situation that prompts this letter. It should be mailed or emailed immediately so that it reaches the person within three to four days. If you wait longer, the letter will have less impact on the situation. Indeed, in the case of the interview thank-you letter, if an employer is making a final hiring decision among three candidates, your letter should arrive as soon as possible to have a chance to affect the outcome.

Whether you handwrite or type this letter may not make a great deal of difference in terms of outcomes, but your choice says something about your professional style and mentality. Many people claim handwritten thank-you letters are more powerful than typed letters. We doubt such claims and have yet to see any credible data on the subject other than personal preferences and questionable logic. It is true that handwritten thank-you letters communicate a certain personal element that cannot be expressed in typewritten letters. If you choose to handwrite this letter, make sure you have attractive handwriting. Poor penmanship could be a negative.

The problem with handwritten letters is that they can express a certain nonprofessional, amateurish style. They also may raise questions about your motivations and manipulative style. They turn off some readers who expect a business letter, rather than an expression of social graces, in reference to a business situation. Furthermore, some readers may consider the handwritten letter an attempt at psychological manipulation – they know what you're trying to do by handwriting a letter. That's what real estate, car, and insurance salespeople are taught to do in their training seminars!

When in doubt, it's best to type this letter in a neat, clean, and professional manner. If typewritten, such a personal letter also will express your professional style and respond to the expectations appropriate for the situation. It tells the reader that you know proper business etiquette; you know this is a business situation, you are equipped to respond, and you attempt to demonstrate your best professional effort.

However, if you are still incarcerated, you may need to handwrite your letters since you do not have access to a computer or typewriter. If this is your situation, try to write as neatly as possible and on the most professional looking paper available. Your situation is not ideal for projecting the best professional image possible, but you can at least put your best foot forward.

The seven thank-you letters appearing on pages 170 through 176 illustrate the different types of thank-you letters that may be sent when conducting a job search. They stress how "thanks" can be expressed in a very professional manner that makes a very positive impression on the reader. These letters – along with the writers – tend to be remembered by the letter recipients.

Thank-You Letter Examples

The following examples of various types of thank-you letters should give you some important ideas on how to write your own thank-you letters in the days and weeks ahead. After reviewing these letters, identify 10 people to whom you might want to write a thank-you letter to during the next 10 days. These should be people who might become important to your job search. Again, try to "think outside the box" by also identifying people whom you may not have a very good relationship with. In some cases, your thank-you letter may take the form of asking forgiveness while also thanking the individual for even small favors.

Try to identify the positive in other people as you write these unique and powerful letters.

Name	Type of Thank-You Letter
1. _____	_____
2. _____	_____
3. _____	_____
4. _____	_____
5. _____	_____
6. _____	_____
7. _____	_____
8. _____	_____
9. _____	_____
10. _____	_____

Thank-You Letter
(referral)

9821 West Fulton Street
Miami, FL 30303

March 7, 20___

Martin Davis
213 Doreen Drive
Miami, FL 30301

Dear Martin,

Thanks so much for putting me in contact with Jane Burton at Fordham Manufacturing Company.

I spoke with her today about my interests in technical training. She was most gracious with her time and provided me with a great deal of useful information on job opportunities in the Miami area. She even made some valuable suggestions for strengthening my resume and gave me a few names of individuals who might be interested in my qualifications.

I'll send you a copy of my resume once I revise it. Please feel free to make any comments or suggestions as well as share it with others who might be interested in my background.

Again, thanks so much for putting me in contact with Jane Burton. She spoke very highly of you and your work with the United Fund.

Sincerely,

Steven Zolbert

Steven Zolbert

Thank-You Letter

(after informational interview)

1289 Fourth Street
St. Louis, MO 62011

March 4, 20___

Jeff Allen, President
ALLEN CONSTRUCTION COMPANY
7128 Eastern Boulevard
St. Louis, MO 62111

Dear Mr. Allen:

Your advice was most helpful in clarifying my questions about careers in construction. I am now reworking my resume and have included many of your thoughtful suggestions. I will send you a copy next week.

Thanks so much for taking time from your busy schedule to see me. I will keep in contact and follow through on your suggestion to see Mel Thompson about opportunities with A. C. Wright Construction Company.

Sincerely,

Tom Wilkerson

Tom Wilkerson

Thank-You Letter
(post job interview)

> 728 Westfields Drive
> Jackson, MS 31222
>
> September 2, 20__
>
>
> Emily Goodman
> Director, Personnel Department
> Jason-Pier Manufacturing Company
> 157 Battlefield Drive
> Jackson, MS 31222
>
>
> Dear Ms. Goodman:
>
> Thank you again for the opportunity to interview for the warehouse position. I appreciated your hospitality and enjoyed meeting you and Tom Wilson.
>
> The interview convinced me of how compatible my background, interests, and skills are with the goals of Jason-Pier Manufacturing. My prior warehouse experience with Ace Hardware and my recent work with the State of Mississippi have prepared me well for this warehouse position. I am confident my work could result in increased savings for your company.
>
> I look forward to meeting you and your staff again.
>
> Sincerely,
>
> *Steven Reed*
>
> Steven Reed

Thank-You Letter
(responding to rejection)

341 Grand Street West
Boston, MA 01101

October 1, 20___

Dan Shields
Vice President for Sales
SANFORD ENTERPRISES
391 Massachusetts Avenue
Boston, MA 01101

Dear Mr. Shields:

Thank you for giving me the opportunity to interview for the Customer Services Representative position. I appreciate your consideration and interest in me. I learned a great deal from our meetings.

Although I am disappointed in not being selected for your current vacancy, I want you to know that I appreciated the courtesy and professionalism shown to me during the entire selection process. I enjoyed meeting you, Stephanie Coates, and other members of your sales staff. My meetings confirmed that Sanford Enterprises would be an exciting place to work and build a career.

Since I am very interested in working with you, please keep me in mind should another position become available in the near future.

Again, thank you for the opportunity to interview. Best wishes to you and your staff.

Yours truly,

Eric Connors

Eric Connors

Thank-You Letter

(withdrawing from consideration)

733 Main Street
Norfolk, VA 23455

December 1, 20____

Tom Billings
Stevens Trucking Company
2500 Military Highway
Norfolk, VA 23456

Dear Tom,

It was indeed a pleasure meeting with you last week to discuss your need for a dispatcher in your Norfolk office. Our time together was most enjoyable and informative.

After careful consideration, I have decided to withdraw from consideration for the position.

My decision is based opon several factors. First, the late evening and weekend hours conflict with my family and church responsibilities. Second, since this is a part-time position with no health benefits, I would not be able to afford health insurance, which is essential for me and my family. Third, the position does not appear to lead to full-time position and advancement within your company.

While I'm sure I would do an excellent job for you, I just wished the position were a better fit for my skills and professional interests.

I want to thank you for interviewing me and giving me the opportunity to learn about your needs. You have a fine staff, and I would have enjoyed working for them.

Sincerely,

James Laramie

James Laramie

Thank-You Letter

(accepting job offer)

2891 Tremont Court
Detroit, MI 48771

December 10, 20___

Gerald McDonald
Vice President
MIDWEST AIRLINES
2211 Vincent Highway
Detroit, MI 48821

Dear Mr. McDonald,

I am pleased to accept your offer, and I am looking forward to joining you and your staff next month.

The customer relations position is ideally suited to my background and interests. I assure you I will give you my best effort in making this an effective position within your company.

I understand I will begin work on December 18. If, in the meantime, I need to complete any paperwork or take care of any other matters, please contact me at 789-377-4029.

I enjoyed meeting with you and your staff and appreciated the professional matter in which the hiring was conducted.

Sincerely,

Jed Owens

Jed Owens

Thank-You Letter

(terminating employment)

1099 Seventh Avenue
Akron, OH 44522

August 2, 20____

Mr. James T. Thomas
Chief Engineer
AKRON CONSTRUCTION CO.
1170 South Hills Highway
Akron, OH 44524

Dear Jim,

I am writing to inform you that I will be leaving Akron Construction Company on September 12 to accept another position.

As you know, I have developed an interest in architectural drafting which combines my drafting skills with my artistic interests. While I was vacationing in Houston recently, a relative approached me about an opening for someone with my background with a large architecture and engineering firm. I investigated the possibility and, consequently, received an offer. After careful consideration, I decided to accept the offer and relocate to Houston. I will be working with Brown and Little Company.

I have thoroughly enjoyed working with you over the past two years, and deeply appreciate your fine supervision and support. You have taught me a great deal about drafting, and I want to thank you for providing me with the opportunity to work here. It has been a very positive experience for me both personally and professionally.

I wanted to give you more than the customary two weeks notice so you would have time to find my replacement. I made the decision to relocate yesterday and decided to inform you immediately.

Best wishes.

Sincerely,

John Albert

John Albert

10

Other Letters for Managing Your Job Search

W
HILE COVER LETTERS AND thank-you letters are two of the most important letters you need to write when looking for a job, you should also be aware of six other types of job search letters. These letters should be written at various stages of your job search and normally are **not** accompanied by a resume. These letters promote your candidacy in many different and effective ways.

In this chapter we introduce you to various letters you may want to write as you launch your job search. Most of these letters are written prior to sending your resume to prospective employers. In fact, some of these letters can be written while incarcerated. We briefly explain each type of letter and include a few examples of the various letters. For numerous examples of these letters, see Ron and Caryl Krannich's *201 Dynamite Job Search Letters* (Impact Publications, 2005).

Additional Job Search Letters

As you begin organizing your job search, be prepared to write these types of job search letters in addition to cover and thank-you letters:

1. **Start-up letters:** These are information-gathering letters designed to learn more about the job market, employers, organizations, jobs, job searches,

relocation considerations, and resources for managing your job search. While much of this information can be accessed by telephone, well-crafted letters will go a long way in launching a successful job search at this initial stage. Examples of such letters appear on pages 180-184.

2. **Laying the groundwork letters:** These letters are designed to develop important relationships for conducting an effective job search. Most of these letters are addressed to people you know but who may not be aware you are in the process of looking for a job. Examples of these letters appear on pages 185-188.

3. **Networking and approach letters:** These letters are designed to develop important contacts and job leads. While application and cover letters primarily respond to want ads or vacancy announcements, these letters are usually not written with a particular job vacancy in mind. Their purpose is to **develop contacts** which may or may not lead to useful information, advice, and referrals. Eventually many of these letters pay off by making contacts with employers who have jobs appropriate for your interests, skills, and abilities. Examples of these letters appear on pages 189-191.

4. **Resume letters:** These letters are usually written in lieu of the traditional cover letter/resume combination. As such, a resume letter incorporates the experience sections of your resume in the format of an approach or application letter. Resume letters have one major advantage over the more traditional letter-resume combination: they enable the writer to customize a resume and letter in reference to the specific needs of employers. Examples of these letters appear on pages 192-195.

5. **Follow-up letters:** While the most efficient and effective follow-up method will be the telephone, on occasion you may want to write follow-up letters to be mailed, faxed, or emailed to your contacts. This normally occurs when you cannot get a phone number, or the letter recipient does not return your phone call after repeated attempts to contact them. These letters are initiated by you in an attempt to get the letter recipient to take action related to the content of your letter. Examples of these letters appear on pages 196-200.

6. **Special and unusual letters:** These letters go beyond the conventional letters represented in this book. They operate on the edge of what is considered to be acceptable job search communication. Not expecting to receive such communication from job seekers, employers react to unconventional letters in different ways. Impressed by the writer's creativity, entrepreneurism, and drive, many employers remember, interview, and hire such candidates. Other employers are turned off by the aggressive and sometime silly nature of such letters. Whatever the reaction, for better or for worse, these letters do grab the attention of letter recipients and can be extremely effective in the "right" situations. Examples of these letters appear on pages 201-204.

Requesting Information
(relocation)

882 Timberlake Road
Minneapolis, MN 54371

February 7, 20____

Janice Watson
APARTMENT FINDERS
792 North Adams Street
Suite 319
Knoxville, TN 38921

Dear Ms. Watson:

I plan to move to the Knoxville area within the next six months.
Please send me information on your services as well as sample
copies of current listings. I would also appreciate any information on Knoxville that would help me better understand the
community, such as a directory of churches, schools, and community activities.

I am especially interested in finding a neighborhood with good
schools and recreational facilities.

I look forward to working with you in the coming weeks.

Sincerely,

Steven Pollock

Steven Pollock

Developing Connections
(long-distance employers)

771 West Nelson St.
Denver, CO 80121

May 14, 20____

President
CHAMBER OF COMMERCE
444 State Avenue
Phoenix, AZ 89921

Dear President:

I will be moving to the Phoenix area soon. I would appreciate it if you could send me a directory of your members. I'm especially interested in making contact with retailers who are the major employers in your community.

Thank you for your assistance.

Sincerely,

Stephanie Adams

Stephanie Adams

Requesting Information/Registering
(temporary employment services)

1134 Stanford Lane
Orlando, FL 31339
July 11, 20___

Janice Eaton
HIGH TEMPS
73 Weston Road
Suite 913
Orlando, FL 31341

Dear Ms. Eaton:

I am interested in a temporary position in word processing. As my enclosed resume indicates, I have over seven years of progressively responsible experience working with a variety of software programs. During the past three years I have extensively used the newest versions of Word.

Could you please send me information on how I might work with your organization? I assume you have signed contracts with those who register with your firm. Please send me information about your organization as well as the necessary forms for registration.

I would appreciate it if you could keep my resume on file for future reference. Should a position become available for someone with my experience, I would like to hear from you.

I will give you a call next week to answer any questions you might have concerning my interests and background.

Sincerely,

Martin Davis

Martin Davis

Requesting Information
(job search services)

8901 Taylor Road
Birmingham, AL 32112

April 2, 20___

Alice Steves, Director
THE WOMEN'S CENTER
7742 Federal Avenue
Birmingham, AL 32114

Dear Ms. Steves:

I learned from a recent article in the Daily News that you offer job and career assistance. Since I've been out of the job market for several years, I'm really interested in learning about job alternatives for someone with my background. I also need to get a better idea of what I'm best qualified to do as well as how to write a resume.

Could you please send me information on the services available through your center? For example, do you offer individualized testing and assessment services and courses on how to write resumes and interview for jobs? I would be interested in knowing how I can best use the Women's Center for conducting a job search.

I appreciate your assistance and look forward to working with you and your staff.

Sincerely,

Janice Furniss

Janice Furniss

Requesting Assistance
(job search services)

1134 West Ford Ave.
Dallas, TX 73112

August 14, 20____

Dr. Delores Clements
DALLAS COMMUNITY COLLEGE
Career Counseling Center
241 Lone Star Blvd.
Dallas, TX 73110

Dear Dr. Clements:

A friend informed me that your Center offers a variety of job search courses and services that are open to the general public.

I've been unemployed during the past three months. So far my efforts at landing a job have not been successful. At this point I think I need some professional guidance to help get my job search on track.

Could you send me information on what types of courses and services you offer? I probably need some testing and assessment work. And I know I could use some assistance on improving my resume.

Sincerely,

Martin Morrison

Martin Morrison

Requesting References
(minister)

Martin Feiler, #17984832
Atlee State Prison
Route 3, Box 402
Atlee, NC 33261

March 19, 20____

Rev. George C. Allen
CHURCH OF CHRIST
984 Angelical Avenue
Winston-Salem, NC 39482

Dear Rev. Allen:

As you may know, I will be released from Atlee State Prison in June after serving three years for drug possession. During that time I was able to turn my life around by participating in various self-development programs and devoting my life to Christ. I also completed my GED and earned several hours toward an Associates Degree through North Carolina Community College. I've hoping to eventually complete a Bachelor's degree in Business Administration.

I will be actively looking for job as soon as I am released. If all goes well, I hope to land a job that will allow me to work part time on my degree. My goal is to eventually work for one of the major commercial real estate firms in Winston-Salem.

Would you be so kind as to serve as a personal reference? Since I have very little work experience, potential employers will probably want to know something about my personal character. I thought of you as a reference because I was once active in our church youth group. I believe you more than anyone else have had a chance to observe me working with others and you are familiar with my background.

I appreciate your assistance. Should an employer ask for a reference, I will give them your name and telephone number.

Sincerely,

Martin Feiler

Martin Feiler

Requesting Advice and Referrals

GERALD S. SNYDER　　　　　　Email: snyderg@earthweb.net
782 South Street　■　Seattle, WA 98322　■　802-731-9228

August 3, 20___

John Turner
CUSTOM CONSTRUCTION
993 Colony Terrace
Seattle, WA 98321

Dear John,

I wanted to let you know that I'm in the process of looking for a job. Since my release from Washington State Prison last month, I moved back with my family here in Seattle. I've been busy these last two weeks just getting adjusted to my new life on the outside. It has been great getting re-acquainted with my family and renewing old friendships. Everyone has been very supportive of my desire to move on with my life.

Now it's time that I start looking for a job that would best utilize my carpentry skills. With the recent construction boom in this area, I'm sure several employers could use my framer skills.

Do you know of any employers in the Seattle area that would be interested in my construction experience? Perhaps you might have some suggestions as to whom I might contact. I enclose a copy of my resume for your reference.

I'll give you a call next week.

Sincerely,

Gerald Snyder

Gerald Snyder

Expressing Gratitude for Job Search Advice

9912 Cortney Place
Alexandria, VA 20999
March 2, 20____

Sarah Allison
839 P Street, NW
Washington, DC 20032

Dear Sarah,

Thanks so much for your advice on contacting nonprofit organizations dealing with homeless shelters and community housing. I never had an idea there were so many such organizations in the Washington, DC area. Indeed, your advice on how to locate such employers opened up a whole new world of employment possibilities!

What a pleasant surprise it was to discover that several of the organizations were located in Alexandria, Virginia, which is near where I live. After making a few contacts, I learned that many of these organizations hire ex-offenders who can work with disadvantaged groups. My strong organization and communication skills should be of interest to such employers.

I've contacted several nonprofits in the Washington, DC and Northern Virginia during the past few days. The ones that most interest me are doing exciting work in organizing community organizations in public housing projects. I'm developing some good contacts with these organizations that I hope will turn into job interviews.

Without your advice I would have overlooked so many potential employers related to my interests and skills. Thanks for helping me re-direct my job search focus. I'll keep you posted as to where all this leads.

Sincerely,

James Patterson

James Patterson
pattersonj@ace.com

Expressing Gratitude for Job Referral

8123 Park Avenue
Albuquerque, NM 84913
May 17, 20____

Vivien Parker
452 Albert Street
Albuquerque, NM 84909

Dear Vivien,

You were right! Margaret Easton knows her stuff. What a wonderful person to meet and learn from.

She was really helpful in giving me advice on whom to contact for possible job openings in the hospitality and entertainment industries. She also shared some of her "inside" observations on which hotels and casinos I should avoid. I did not know, for example, that some properties in Albuquerque are currently reducing their staffs whereas others in Santa Fe and Taos are actually experiencing significant expansion.

She suggested that I focus my job search on a few small properties. She made some good suggestions on how I could best strengthen my resume for such companies. She also referred me to three condominium complexes in Santa Fe which I've contacted; two will interview me next week.

I enclose a copy of my revised resume for your reference. I think it better represents my goals than the one I gave you a few weeks ago.

Thanks again for recommending that I contact Ms. Easton for information and advice. She may be responsible for my landing my next job!

Sincerely,

Jack Davidson

Jack Davidson
jdavidson@hotmail.com

Referral
(Information and advice)

1099 Seventh Avenue
Akron, OH 44522
December 10, 20___

Janet L. Cooper, Director
Architectural Design Office
RT ENGINEERING ASSOCIATES
621 West Grand Avenue
Akron, OH 44520

Dear Ms. Cooper:

John Sayres suggested that I write to you regarding my interest in architectural drafting. He thought you would be a good person to give me some career advice.

I am interested in an architectural drafting position with a firm specializing in commercial construction. As a trained draftsman, I have six years of progressive experience in all facets of construction, from pouring concrete to developing plans for $14 million in commercial and residential construction. I am particularly interested in improving construction design and building operations of shopping complexes.

Mr. Sayres mentioned you as one of the leading experts in this growing field. Would it be possible for us to meet briefly? Over the next few months I will be conducting a job search. I am certain your counsel would assist me as I begin looking for new opportunities.

I will call your office next week to see if your schedule permits such a meeting.

Sincerely,

John Albert

John Albert
jalbert@hotmail.com

Cold Turkey
(Information and advice)

2189 West Church Street
New York, NY 10011

May 3, 20___

Patricia Dotson, Director
NORTHEAST ASSOCIATION FOR THE ELDERLY
9930 Jefferson Street
New York, NY 10013

Dear Ms. Dotson:

I have been impressed with your work with the elderly. Your organization takes a community perspective in trying to integrate the concerns of the elderly with those of other community groups. Perhaps other organizations will soon follow your lead.

I am anxious to meet you and learn more about your work. My background with the city Volunteer Services Program involved frequent contact with elderly volunteers. From this experience I decided I preferred working primarily with the elderly.

However, before I pursue my interest further, I need to talk to people with experience in gerontology. In particular, I would like to know more about careers with the elderly as well as how my background might best be used in the field of gerontology.

I am hoping you can assist me in this matter. I would like to meet with you briefly to discuss several of my concerns. I will call next week to see if your schedule permits such a meeting.

I look forward to meeting you.

Sincerely,

Carol Timms

Carol Timms
ctimms@yahoo.com

Referral
(possible opening)

485 High Bluff Road
Santa Fe, NM 89543
October 3, 20 _____

Rebecca Lyons
WESTERN INDUSTRIES, INC.
98347 W. Main Street
Albuquerque, NM 89977

Dear Mrs. Lyons:

Cynthia Pringle, my current supervisor and one of your acquaintances, suggested I write to you. I will be relocating to Albuquerque within the next six weeks and will be looking for employment as a secretary. Cynthia indicated your firm is frequently in need of dependable and competent people to fill vacancies.

I have worked for Cynthia for the past three years and have consistently received "outstanding" ratings in all areas on my performance evaluations. I get along well with people and look forward to beginning work in a new firm in my new city.

I will be driving into Albuquerque the week of the 15th and hope I might be able to meet with you at that time. Even if you do not have a vacancy or anticipate one at this time, I would appreciate the opportunity to talk with you about other contacts I might make to further my job search in Albuquerque.

I will call you next week and hope we may be able to schedule a meeting. I will appreciate any assistance you may be able to give me and look forward to meeting you. Cynthia speaks so highly of you that I know your assistance would be truly valuable to me.

Sincerely,

Karen Jostney

Karen Jostney
kjostney@yahoo.com

Vacancy Announcement
(Sales/Information Processing)

136 West Davis St.
Sacramento, CA 98771

September 5, 20____

Vicki Beatress
S.R. SYSTEMS
893 Mountain View Road
Sacramento, CA 98777

Dear Ms. Beatress:

I read with interest your ad in today's *Sacramento Star* for a Sales Associate. I'm especially interested in this position because of my previous experience in working with copy machines and corporate clients. I have been both a user and promoter of your systems.

My experience and qualifications include seven years of progressive experience in the following positions:

- <u>Sales Associate</u>: Represented both Toshiba and Ricoh copy machines to corporate clients. Increased corporate accounts by 30% within 18 months. Recognized as the top Toshiba salesperson for the past three years. Linotech Systems.

- <u>Office Manager</u>: Performed office management responsibilities. Planned and re-organized service center. Initiated time and cost studies which saved company $40,000 in additional labor costs. MCT Corporation.

I also recently completed my bachelor's degree in business administration, with an emphasis on marketing.

I believe my interests, skills, and experience are a good fit for this position. May I call you on Wednesday afternoon to answer any questions you may have concerning my candidacy?

Sincerely,

Wayne Watson

Wayne Watson
<u>watsonw@aol.com</u>

Vacancy Announcement
(Architectural Drafter)

1099 Seventh Avenue
Akron, OH 44522
February 1, 20___

Michael Abrams
THE LIGHTNER COMPANY
8113 Grand Avenue
Akron, OH 44520

Dear Mr. Abrams:

I am very interested in the Architectural Drafter position you advertised in today's *Akron Beacon Journal*. This is exactly the type of position I have been seeking. It fits nicely with my technical knowledge and practical experience for enhancing construction design and building operations.

I would bring to this position nearly 10 years of responsible experience in all phases of construction design:

- <u>Draftsman</u>: Akron Construction Company, Akron. Helped develop construction plans for $14 million of residential and commercial construction.

- <u>Drafting Assistant/Apprentice</u>: R.T. Design Company, Akron. Served as an apprentice in helping design residential developments. Worked on the $130 million Lakeview Estate Development Center.

- <u>Cabinetmaker</u>: Jason's Linoleum and Carpet Company, Akron. Designed and constructed kitchen countertops and cabinets; installed the material in homes; cut and laid linoleum flooring in apartment complexes.

- <u>Carpenter's Assistant</u>: Kennison Associates, Akron. Assisted carpenter in the reconstruction of a restaurant and in building forms for pouring concrete.

My training background includes completion of 15 hours of drafting courses at the Akron Vocational and Training Center.

I appreciate your consideration. I will call you on Monday afternoon to answer any questions you may have about my candidacy.

Sincerely,

John Albert

John Albert
albertj@aol.com

Vacancy Announcement
(Bookkeeper)

997 Mountain Road
Denver, CO 80222
June 4, 20___

James Fountain
SIMON WALTERS, INC.
771 George Washington Blvd.
Denver, CO 80220

Dear Mr. Fountain:

I read with interest your ad in today's *Rocky Mountain Times* for a book-keeper. I believe my experience may be ideally suited for this position:

- **Manager, Accounts Payable, T.L. Dutton, Denver**: Supervised 18 employees who routinely processed 200 invoices a day. Handled vendor inquiries and adjustments. Conducted quarterly accruals and reconciliations. Screened candidates and conducted annual performance evaluations. Reduced the number of billing errors by 30 percent and vendor inquiries by 25 percent within the first year.

- **Supervisor, Accounts Payable, AAA Pest Control, Denver**: Supervised 10 employees who processed nearly 140 invoices a day. Audited vendor invoices, authorized payments, and balanced daily disbursements. Introduced automated accounts receivable system for improving the efficiency and accuracy of receivables.

- **Bookkeeper, Davis Nursery, Ft. Collins**: Processed accounts payable and receivable, reconciled accounts, balanced daily disbursements, and managed payroll for a 20-employee organization with annual revenues of $1.8 million.

- **Bookkeeper, Jamison's Lumber, Ft. Collins**: Assisted accountant in processing accounts payable and receivable and managing payroll for a 40-employee organization with annual revenues of $3.2 million.

I am currently taking advanced courses in accounting, computer science, and management at Colorado Junior College in Denver.

I will call you on Thursday afternoon to answer any questions you may have concerning my candidacy.

Sincerely,

Joe Barrows

Joe Barrows
barrowsj@erols.com

Broadcast
(Construction)

1131 N. Bridge Road
Baltimore, MD 21027

December 7, 20___

I am interested in an construction management/supervision position with a growing design/build firm. My experience includes:

- <u>Management</u>: Owner and President for 14 years of a design/build firm with annual revenues between $1 million and $2 million.

- <u>Construction</u>: Direct experience with most methodologies of construction including wood frame, masonry, and light metal.

- <u>Supervision</u>: Responsible for 15 full-time employees. Concurrently supervised several hundred sub-contractors/crews. Many crews were non-English speaking.

- <u>Architectural design</u>: Residential experience with custom and track family homes ranging from 1,000 to 10,000 square feet. Commercial experience with retail, office, office/warehouse, warehouse, restaurants, and marinas.

If my interests, skills, and experience coincide with your hiring needs, I would appreciate hearing from you. I can be contacted at 301-111-0981.

Sincerely,

George Willington

George Willington

Placement Assistance
(Follow-up)

246 Cathedral Drive
Salt Lake City, UT 86732

July 15, 20____

James Martin
Association Referral Service
U.S. CHAMBER OF COMMERCE
1615 H Street, NW
Washington, DC 20062

Dear Mr. Martin:

Did you get my letter of June 3? Assuming it got lost along the way, I enclose a copy of the original for your reference.

I am interested in receiving information on employment opportunities in Western Europe. For your convenience, I enclose a self-addressed stamped envelope. I also can be reached at 818-839-9193 or vertimosas@ace.com.

Many thanks for your assistance.

Sincerely,

Sandra Vertimosa

Sandra Vertimosa
vertimosas@ace.com

Vacancy Announcement
(Follow-up)

136 West Davis St.
Sacramento, CA 98771

September 15, 20___

Vicki Beatress
S.R. SYSTEMS
893 Mountain View Road
Sacramento, CA 98777

Dear Ms. Beatress:

On September 5, I sent you a copy of the attached letter in application for a Sales Associate position. Have you had a chance to make any preliminary decisions?

I want to reiterate my interest in this position and availability for an interview. I believe my interests, skills, and experience are an excellent fit for this position.

I will call you next Thursday to answer any questions you may have about my candidacy.

Sincerely,

Wayne Watson

watsonw@aol.com

Interview Confirmation
(Follow-up)

1234 Main Street
Norfolk, VA 23508

April 30, 20____

Dale Roberts
Business Manager
VIRGINIA BEACH
    CONVENTION CENTER
2981 Ocean Boulevard
Virginia Beach, VA 23519

Dear Mr. Roberts:

Just a quick note to reconfirm our appointment next Tuesday at 10:30am. I look forward to discussing with you how my interests, skills, and experience can promote the Virginia Beach Convention Center.

As you requested, I enclose a copy of my resume for your reference. Please let me know if you need any additional information before our meeting on Tuesday.

Sincerely,

Karen Jones

Karen Jones
karenjones@earthone.com

Vacancy Announcement
(Follow-up)

997 Mountain Road
Denver, CO 80222

June 11, 20___

James Fountain
SIMON WALTERS, INC.
771 George Washington Blvd.
Denver, CO 80220

Dear Mr. Fountain:

I'm not doing well in the telephone department. I called your office but was unable to get through to you.

I was just following up on my letter of June 4 in application for the bookkeeper position you had advertised in last week's *Rocky Mountain Times*. Have you had a chance to review my application? I also wanted to let you know that I am still interested in this position and would appreciate an opportunity to meet with you to discuss how my interests, skills, and experience can best contribute to sound financial reporting at Simon Walters, Inc.

I'll try to call you again next Tuesday. Perhaps your schedule will be less hectic by that time.

Sincerely,

Jane Barrows

Jane Barrows
barrowsj@erols.com

Vacancy Announcement
(Follow-up)

717 Georgia Avenue
Indianapolis, IN 48712

March 9, 20___

Barry Bates
Human Resources
GREATER INDIANAPOLIS HOSPITAL
67100 Conners Road
Indianapolis, IN 48712

Dear Mr. Bates:

Thanks so much for returning my call today. I appreciated your
thoughtfulness and learned a great deal about your needs and
the nature of the Occupational Therapist position.

As you requested, I instructed my university placement office to
send you a copy of my file. It includes transcripts, three letters of
recommendation, and a sample of my work. Since I requested
these documents be sent to you by Federal Express, they should
reach you within two days.

I'll give you a call next week to answer any additional questions
you may have about my interest in this position.

Sincerely,

Susan Wright

Susan Wright
wrights@aol.com

Special and Unusual Letters

**AUTOMOTIVE
WAREHOUSE NEWS**

For Immediate Release
Tel. 919-738-2981

Innovative Warehouse Inventory System Reduces Labor Costs By 35%!

Yes, it's true. A newly installed inventory system reduced labor costs by 35% at J. L. Automotive Parts. Mark Timpson, an employee with over seven years experience in parts management, developed an innovative inventory system custom-designed to meet the growing demand for used antique car parts. *"It really wasn't as difficult as I thought,"* Mark explains. *"I worked with a fine team of professionals who really know the parts business. We put our heads together over a three-week period to create a new computerized system that reduced our labor costs by 35% within eight months."*

For his team efforts, Mark received the Employee of the Year award. He believes this system is easily adapted to other automotive parts businesses and warehouse operations. He's prepared to demonstrate this approach to parties interested in strengthening their warehouse management systems.

#   #   #

For further information, including a detailed resume, or for scheduling an interview or demonstration, contact:

Mark Timpson
1873 Tyson Road
San Diego, CA 98712
Tel. 919-738-2981
timpsonm@aol.com
www.marktimpson.com

Shoe-In-The-Box
(Resume inserted in shoe)

ANGEL ROBERTS   robertsa@aol.com   819 Collier Drive
San Jose, CA 94011 ▪ 917-371-9021 ▪ July 19, 20___

Milton Whitehead
Director of Sales
SATURN PHARMACEUTICAL CO.
7213 American Drive
St. Louis, MO 63811

Dear Mr. Whitehead:

Now that I have my shoe in the door, how about an interview?

Expecting a call,

Angel Roberts

Angel Roberts

Enclosures: Angel's right shoe with resume stuffed inside

Telegram or E-mail

RESUME ARRIVING TOMORROW NOON BY FEDERAL EXPRESS. PLEASE EXAMINE CAREFULLY. CANDIDATE (SHEILA WATSON) WITH THREE YEARS EXPERIENCE DEVELOPING HIGHLY SUCCESSFUL ART LEASING PROGRAM WISHES TO INTERVIEW FOR RECENTLY ADVERTISED LEASING MANAGER POSITION. ENCLOSING SAMPLE BROCHURES AND STRATEGIC MARKETING PLAN FOR YOUR REVIEW. EXPECTING EXCELLENT MARKET IN SECOND HALF OF YEAR BASED ON RECENT ANALYSIS OF CORPORATE ART ACQUISITION PATTERNS. WILLING TO TRAVEL AND RELOCATE. CALL 317-378-9871, FAX 317-378-8712, OR EMAIL WATSONS@ACE.COM FOR MORE INFORMATION OR APPOINTMENT.

3 x 5 Announcement Card

Where can you find fresh talent for promoting renewable energy resource issues?

I may be just out of college, but I have something most other college graduates lack – three years of environmental activism at both the state and local levels. I love producing results that contribute to protecting the environment. By June of next year, I want to be your most effective lobbyist throughout California.

You'll find my resume on the back of this card. Let's talk soon. I think we could work well together on issues we both are committed to seeing translated into public policy.

CONTACT: Janet Trueblood
Tel. 216-332-3829
truebloodj@aol.com

11

Production, Distribution, and Follow-Up Issues

WHILE IT IS IMPORTANT TO write outstanding resumes and letters, you also need to deal with several key production, distribution, and follow-up issues. The effectiveness of your resume or letter is only as good as the quality of your production, distribution, and follow-up activities.

Now that you have written your resume or letter, what will you do next? How will you produce it? How do you plan to get it into the hands of the right people who have the power to hire? What are the best ways to distribute a resume or letter to ensure it has its intended impact? How can you make sure it gets read and responded to? Are there certain things you can do to increase the probability that you will be invited to a job interview? These and many other questions relate to important production, distribution, and follow-up issues you need to address in addition to "just" writing your resume and letters.

Production

Employers also want to see your best professional effort at the production stage of resume and letter writing. This involves making the right choices about paper color, weight, and texture as well as production methods. Above all, the resume and letter they receive must be error-free, or they are likely to discard it as an example of incompetence.

The production of your resumes and letters should follow these five principles:

1. **Carefully proofread and print out two or three drafts of your communication before producing the final copies.** Be sure to carefully proofread for grammatical, spelling, and punctuation errors before producing the final camera-ready copy. Assuming you are word processing your resume and letters, be sure to run the spell-check and grammar programs. Any spelling, grammatical, or punctuation errors will quickly disqualify you with employers. Read and reread the draft several times to see if you can improve various elements to make it more readable and eye appealing. Read for both form and content. Have someone else also review your resume or letter and give you feedback on its form and content. Use the evaluation forms in Chapter 12 to conduct both internal and external evaluations. They are critical!

2. **Choose white, off-white, ivory, or light gray 20 to 25 lb. bond paper with 100% cotton fiber ("rag content").** Your choice of paper – color, weight, and texture – does make a difference to readers. It says something about your professional style. Choose a poor quality paper and inappropriate color and you communicate the wrong message to employers. There is nothing magical about ivory or off-white paper. As more and more people use these colors, off-white and ivory have probably lost their distinction. To be different, try a light gray or basic white. Indeed, white paper gives a nice, bright, and crisp look to what has become essentially a dull-colored process. Stay with black ink or use dark navy ink on light gray paper. If you are applying for a creative position, you may decide to use more daring colors to better express your creative style and personality. However, stay away from dark-colored papers. Resumes should have a light, bright look to them. The paper should also match your cover letter and envelope.

3. **Produce your resume and letters on 8½ x 11" paper.** This is the standard business size that you should follow. Other sizes are too unconventional and thus communicate the wrong message to readers. Make sure the envelope matches the size of the paper.

4. **Print only on one side of the paper.** Do not produce a two-sided resume. If your resume runs two pages, print it on two separate pages and staple

them together. Be sure to put your name at the top of the second page, similar to the following header:

Mary Smith	Page 2

5. **Use a good quality machine and an appropriate typeface.** It's best to produce your camera-ready copy (for reproduction) on a letter-quality printer, preferably a laser printer. Avoid manual typewriters that produce uneven type and very amateurish documents. Never produce your resume on a dot matrix printer. Most such printers produce poor quality type that communicates a "mass-production" look. If you use a desktop publishing program, choose serif typefaces (Times Roman, Palatino, New Century). Avoid sans serif typefaces (Gothic, Helvetica, Avant Garde) which are more difficult to read. Be sure you print dark, crisp type.

    Most individuals who lack access to a laser printer reproduce their resume on a copy machine. Indeed, given the high-quality reproduction achieved on many copy machines available at local print shops, it's not necessary to go to the expense of having your resume professionally printed. However, if you need 2,000 or more copies – which is most unlikely unless you resort to a broadcast or "shotgun" marketing approach – it may be more cost effective to have them printed. Just take your camera-ready copy, along with your choice of paper, to a local printer and have them make as many copies as you need. The cost per copy will run anywhere from 3¢ to 15¢, depending on the number of copies run. The larger the run, the cheaper your per unit cost.

Marketing and Distribution

Your resume and letters are only as good as your marketing and distribution efforts. What, for example, will you do with your resume once you've completed it? How can you best get it into the hands of individuals who can make a difference in your job search? Are you planning to send it in response to vacancy announcements and want ads? Maybe you plan to broadcast it to hundreds of employers in the hope someone will call you for an interview? Should you include your resume in the resume databases of various Internet employment sites? Perhaps you only want to send it to a few people who can help you with your job search? Or maybe you really don't have a plan beyond getting it produced in a "correct" form.

Keep the following 12 marketing and distribution principles in mind as you try to choose the most effective ways of getting your resume and letters in front of the right people:

1. **It's best to target your resume and letters to specific employers rather than broadcast them to hundreds of names and addresses.** Broadcasting or "shotgunning" your resume and letters to hundreds of potential employers will give you a false sense of making progress with your job search since you think you are actually making contact with numerous employers. You will be disappointed with the results. For every 100 resumes you mail, you will be lucky to get one positive response that leads to a job interview. Indeed, many individuals report no responses after mass mailing hundreds of resumes. It's always best to target your resume to specific employers through one or two methods:

    - **Respond to vacancy announcements or want ads.** Resumes sent in response to job listings also will give you a sense of making progress with your job search. Since competition is likely to be high for advertised positions, your chances of getting a job interview may be tough, although much better than if you broadcasted your resume to hundreds of employers who may not have openings.

    - **Target employers with information on your qualifications.** The most effective way of getting job interviews is to network for information, advice, and referrals. You do this by contacting friends, professional associates, acquaintances, and others who might have information on jobs related to your interests and skills. You, in effect, attempt to uncover job vacancies before they become publicized or meet an employment need not yet recognized by employers, who may then create a position for you in line with your qualifications.

        The resume plays an important role in this networking process. In some cases, you will be referred to someone who is interested in seeing your resume; when that happens, send it along with a cover letter and follow up your mailing with a telephone call. In other cases, you will conduct informational interviews with individuals who can give you advice and referrals relevant to your career interests. You should take your resume to the informational interview and at the very end of your meeting ask your informant to critique your resume. In the process of examining your resume, your informant is likely to give you good feedback for further revising your resume as well as refer you and your resume to others. If you regularly repeat this networking and informational interviewing process, within a few weeks you should begin landing job interviews directly related to the qualifications you outlined in your dynamite resume!

2. **If you decide to broadcast your resume, the best way to do so is to enter it into resume databases, post it on online bulletin boards, or use resume blasting services.** We view the resume databases operated by various Internet employment sites as a new form of high-tech resume broadcasting. Resumes in these databases, which can contain between 500 and 50,000+ resumes, are usually accessed by employers who search for candidates with a particular mix of keywords on their resume. If you have the right combination of skills and experience and know how to write an outstanding resume with language sensitive to the search-and-retrieval software, you should be able to connect with employers through such electronic media.

    At the same time, you may want to use a more traditional direct-mail approach to broadcasting your resume via email – spend from $19.95 to $49.95 on a service to have your resume sent to thousands of employment specialists (primarily recruiters) and websites with resume databases. Dozens of groups, such as www.resumezapper.com and www.resumeagent.com, will broadcast your resume for a fee. However, we do not regard these services as effective ways to distribute a resume. At best, they will give you a false sense of making progress with your job search.

3. **Learn to properly send your resume and letters by email**. More and more employers request that resumes and letters be sent to them by email rather than by regular mail or by fax. The principles for producing and distributing (formatting, typestyle, etiquette, etc.) an emailed resume differ from those relevant for a paper resume sent by mail or faxed. If you communicate a great deal with employers on the Internet, you will need to frequently transmit an email version of your resume. Make sure you know how to write and distribute a first-class emailed resume. Here are a few quick tips on the intricacies of emailing resumes:

- If you're going to email your resume as an attachment, be sure to send it in Microsoft Word. Word is the most acceptable format since it is, by far, the most widely used software. If you do not have Word, then consider emailing your resume using one of the other options below.

- If you know that your resume is going to be scanned by a computer, then be sure to email a "plain vanilla" version. What does this mean? Simply put, it means that you need to strip away all of the type enhancements (such as boldface, italics, underlining) and formatting enhancements (for example, boxes, lines, justification) that make your printed resume look nice and, instead, provide a version that can be easily scanned while retaining the integrity of the words on the page. Be sure to put this version of your resume in either **Arial** or **Times Roman** so that it can be read effectively by scanning software.

- If you don't want to send your resume as an attachment (as you would do with the Word and "plain vanilla" versions), then save it as an ASCII text version and paste it into the body of the email message. This will totally eliminate any potential formatting issues that may arise when you email your resume. You can also use this version to paste into online job applications. And, it's easy; simply select "ASCII text" as the format when saving your resume. Although it's not as attractive as a Word version of your resume, there will never be any cause for concern that it did not transmit correctly.

4. **Be prepared to complete online profile forms in lieu of a resume.** Many employers today operate their own online career centers rather than advertise positions in newspapers or through employment websites. Indeed, you are well advised to visit employers' websites for details on employment opportunities, including vacancy announcements and online applications. Candidates complete online applications which often include a candidate profile form that substitutes for a resume. Much of the information requested for completing this form can be taken directly from your resume. You can generally cut and paste sections from your resume into appropriate sections of this form.

5. **Be careful in creating online and video resumes.** Always remember the purpose of a resume — to persuade a hiring manager to invite you to a face-to-face interview. You want to give prospective employers just enough in-

formation to persuade them to invite you to a job interview. Avoid overloading them with lots of unnecessary and potentially negative information. Online resumes often provide too much information to employers. Producers of such resumes also make a faulty assumption – busy employers will actually access their website to view their online creation. Why would they do that when they already spend less than 30 seconds effortlessly browsing a paper resume? Asking someone to visit your website puts new time and effort burdens on them. Video resumes have similar problems. They also include too many verbal and nonverbal elements that should be reserved for a job interview.

6. **Never enclose letters of recommendation, transcripts, or other information with your resume unless requested to do so.** Unsolicited letters of recommendation are negatives. Readers know they have been specially produced to impress them and thus they may question your integrity. Like personal photos, unsolicited transcripts may communicate negative messages, unless you achieved perfect grades. Such information merely detracts from your resume and cover letter; it does not contribute to getting a job interview. It indicates you do not know what you are doing by including such information.

7. **Address your resume to a specific person.** Always try to get the correct name and position of the person who should receive your resume. Unless you are specifically instructed to do so, addressing your correspondence to "Dear Sir/Madam," "Director of Personnel," or "To Whom It May Concern" is likely to result in lost correspondence; the mailroom may treat it as junk mail. If you later follow up your correspondence with a phone call, you have no one to communicate with. A couple of phone calls should quickly result in the proper name. Just call the switchboard or a receptionist and ask the following:

"I need to send some correspondence to the person in charge of _____. Who might that be? What is the spelling of their name? And what is the correct mailing address?"

Keep in mind that the people who have the power to hire are usually not in the Human Resource Office; they tend to be the heads of operating units or hiring managers. Target your resume accordingly!

8. **Don't limit the distribution of your resume and letters only to vacancy announcements.** Your goal should be to get your resume and letters into as many hands as possible. Send them to individuals in your network – your relatives, friends, former colleagues and employers, and anyone else who might be helpful in uncovering job leads. Remember, you want to cast a big net. Let your resume and letters do the fishing by casting them on as many waters as possible.

9. **Enclose your resume and letter in a matching No. 10 business envelope or in a 9 x 12" envelope.** We prefer the 9 x 12" envelope because it keeps your correspondence flat and has a greater impact than the typical No. 10 business envelope. Keep all your stationery matching, including the 9 x 12" envelope. If, however, it's difficult to find a matching 9 x 12" envelope, go with a white or buff-colored envelope or use a U.S. Postal Service "Priority Mail" envelope.

10. **Type the envelope or mailing label rather than handwrite the address.** Handwritten addresses look too personal and amateurish, give off mixed messages, and suggest a subtle form of manipulation on your part. Contrary to what others may tell you, in a job search handwritten addresses – and even handwritten letters or notes – do not gain more attention nor generate more positive responses; they may actually have the opposite effect – label you as being unprofessional or someone who is trying to manipulate the employer with the old handwritten technique. Typed addresses look more professional; they are consistent with the enclosed resume. After all, this is business correspondence, not a social invitation to invite yourself to an interview.

11. **Send your correspondence by first-class or priority mail or special next-day services, and use stamps.** If you want to get the recipient's immediate attention, send your correspondence in one of those colorful next-day air service envelopes provided by the U.S. Postal Service, Federal Express, UPS, or other carriers. However, first-class or priority mail will usually get your correspondence delivered within two to three days. It's best to affix a nice commemorative stamp rather than use a postage meter. A stamp helps personalize your mailing piece and does not raise questions about whose postage meter you used!

12. **Never fax or email your resume and letters unless asked to do so by your recipient.** It is presumptuous for anyone to fax or email their resume or letter to an employer without express permission to do so. Such faxes are treated as junk mail, and emails are viewed as spam and may encounter spam filters; they may be seen as an unwarranted invasion of private channels of communication. If asked to fax or email your correspondence, be sure to follow up by mailing a copy of the original and indicating you sent materials by fax or email on a specific date as requested. The poor quality transmission of many fax machines and the bland look of most email will not do justice to the overall visual quality of your resume. You need a paper follow-up which will also remind the individual of your continuing interest in the position.

Follow-Up

Follow-up remains the least understood but most important step in any job search. Whatever you do, make sure you follow up **all** of your job search activities. If you fail to follow up, you are likely to get little or no response to your job search initiatives. Follow-up means taking action that gets results. Your follow-up should follow these three principles for effectiveness:

1. **Follow up your resume within seven days of mailing it.** Do not let too much time lapse between when you mailed your resume and when you contact the resume recipient. Seven days should give the recipient sufficient time to examine your resume and decide on your future status. If a decision has not been made to interview you, your follow-up action may help accelerate a decision.

2. **The best follow-up for a mailed resume is a telephone call.** Don't expect your resume recipient to take the initiative in calling you for an interview. State in your cover letter that you will call the person at a particular time to discuss your resume. For example,

> I will call your office on the morning of March 17 to see if a meeting can be scheduled at a convenient time.

Then, be sure you follow up with a phone call at the specific time. If you have difficulty contacting the individual, try three times to get through. After the third try, leave a message as well as write a letter as an alternative to the telephone follow-up. In this letter, inquire about the status of your resume, mention your continued interest in the position, and thank the individual for his or her consideration.

3. **Follow up your follow-up with a nice thank-you letter.** Regardless of the outcome of your follow-up phone call, send a nice thank-you letter based on your conversation. You thank the letter recipient for taking the time to speak with you and to reiterate your interest in the position. While some career counselors recommend sending a handwritten thank-you note to personalize communication between you and the employer, we caution against doing so. Remember, you are engaged in a business transaction rather than a social communication. We feel a handwritten letter is inappropriate for such situations. Such a letter should be produced in a typed form and follow the principles of good business correspondence. You can be warm and friendly in what you say. The business letter form keeps you on stage – you are putting your best business foot forward.

12

Evaluating Resumes and Letters

O NCE YOU'VE COMPLETED your resume and letters, you should evaluate each before sending them to anyone who might be interested in your candidacy. In this chapter we include four comprehensive self-evaluation tools for assessing all aspects of your resume and letters. Going beyond writing resumes and letters, this chapter also includes key principles for producing, distributing, and following up resumes and letters.

You should conduct two evaluations: internal and external. With an **internal evaluation**, you examine your resume and letters in reference to a specific checklist of key principles. An **external evaluation** involves having someone else examine your resume and letters for their overall effectiveness.

Importance of Evaluations

Evaluation should play a central role in all of your job search activities. If you want to be most effective, you must continuously evaluate your progress throughout each step of your job search. Evaluation based on specific performance standards eliminates a great deal of wishful thinking that can confuse and misdirect your job search. Best of all, evaluation helps keep your job search focused on goals and productive activities that eventually lead to job interviews and offers.

Internal Resume Evaluation

The first evaluation should take place immediately upon completing the first draft of your resume. Examine your resume in reference to the following statements. Using the numerical ratings below, respond to each statement by circling the appropriate number that most accurately describes your newly crafted resume:

1 = Strongly agree
2 = Agree
3 = So-so
4 = Disagree
5 = Strongly disagree

WRITING

1. Wrote the resume myself – did not copy someone else's resume.   1   2   3   4   5

2. Assessed my interests, skills, and abilities before writing each resume section.   1   2   3   4   5

3. Know how my resume relates to other job search activities, such as networking and interviewing. 1   2   3   4   5

4. Selected an appropriate resume format that best presents my interests, skills, and experience.   1   2   3   4   5

5. Included all essential information categories in the proper order.   1   2   3   4   5

6. Eliminated all extraneous information unrelated to my objective and employers' needs (date, photo, race, religion, political affiliation, age, sex, height, health, hobbies) or better saved for discussion in the job interview – salary history and references.   1   2   3   4   5

7. Put the most important information first.	1	2	3	4	5
8. Resume is oriented to the future rather than to the past.	1	2	3	4	5
9. Contact information is complete – name, address, and phone number. No P.O. Box numbers or nicknames.	1	2	3	4	5
10. Limited abbreviations to a few commonly accepted words.	1	2	3	4	5
11. Contact information attractively formatted to introduce the resume.	1	2	3	4	5
12. Included a thoughtful employer-oriented objective that incorporates both skills and benefits.	1	2	3	4	5
13. Objective clearly communicates to employers what I want to do, can do, and will do for them.	1	2	3	4	5
14. Objective is neither too general nor too specific.	1	2	3	4	5
15. Objective serves as the central organizing element for all other sections of the resume.	1	2	3	4	5
16. Considered including a "Summary of Qualifications" section.	1	2	3	4	5
17. Elaborated work experience in detail, emphasizing my skills, abilities, and achievements.	1	2	3	4	5
18. Each "experience" section is short and to the point.	1	2	3	4	5
19. Consistently used action verbs and the active voice.	1	2	3	4	5
20. Incorporated language appropriate for the keywords of electronic resume scanners.	1	2	3	4	5
21. Did not refer to myself as "I."	1	2	3	4	5

22. Used specifics – numbers and percentages –
    to highlight my performance.   1   2   3   4   5

23. Included positive quotations about my
    performance from previous employers.   1   2   3   4   5

24. Eliminated any negative references,
    including reasons for leaving.   1   2   3   4   5

25. Did not include names of supervisors.   1   2   3   4   5

26. Summarized my most recent job and
    then included other jobs in reverse
    chronological order.   1   2   3   4   5

27. Descriptions of "experience" are consistent.   1   2   3   4   5

28. Put the most important information
    about my skills first when summarizing
    my "experience."   1   2   3   4   5

29. No time gaps nor "job hopping"
    apparent to reader.   1   2   3   4   5

30. Documented "other experience" that
    might strengthen my objective and
    decided to either include or exclude
    it on the resume.   1   2   3   4   5

31. Included complete information on
    my educational background, including
    important highlights.   1   2   3   4   5

32. If had little relevant work experience,
    emphasized educational background
    more than work experience.   1   2   3   4   5

33. Put education in reverse chronological
    order and eliminated high school
    if a college graduate.   1   2   3   4   5

34. Included special education and training
    relevant to my major interests and skills.   1   2   3   4   5

35. Included professional affiliations and
    memberships relevant to my objective and
    skills; highlighted any major contributions. 1   2   3   4   5

36. Documented any special skills not included
    elsewhere on resume,and included those
    that appear relevant to employers' needs.   1   2   3   4   5

37. Included awards or special recognitions
    that further document my skills and
    achievements.   1   2   3   4   5

38. Weighed pros and cons of including a
    personal statement on my resume.   1   2   3   4   5

39. Did not mention salary history or expectations. 1   2   3   4   5

40. Did not include references.   1   2   3   4   5

41. Used language appropriate for the
    employer, including terms that associate
    me with the industry.   1   2   3   4   5

42. My language is crisp, succinct, expressive,
    and direct.   1   2   3   4   5

43. Used type enhancements such as boldface,
    italics, and underlining to make the resume
    most readable.   1   2   3   4   5

44. Resume has an inviting, uncluttered look,
    incorporating sufficient white space and
    using a standard typestyle and size.   1   2   3   4   5

45. Kept the design very basic and conservative.   1   2   3   4   5

46. Kept sentences and sections short and succinct.   1   2   3   4   5

47. Resume runs one or two pages.   1   2   3   4   5

PRODUCTION

48. Carefully proofread and produced two or
    three drafts which were subjected to both
    internal and external evaluations before
    producing the final copies.   1   2   3   4   5

49. Chose a standard color and quality of paper.   1   2   3   4   5

50. Used 8½ x 11" paper.   1   2   3   4   5

51. Printed resume on only one side of paper.   1   2   3   4   5

52. Used a good-quality machine and an
    easy-to-read typeface to print the resume.   1   2   3   4   5

MARKETING AND DISTRIBUTION

53. Targeted resume toward specific employers.   1   2   3   4   5

54. Used resume properly for networking
    and informational interviewing activities.   1   2   3   4   5

55. Posted an electronic version of my resume to
    several resume databases operated by Internet
    employment sites as well as explored

    numerous bulletin boards, discussion groups,
and employer sites on the Internet.   1   2   3   4   5

56. Know how to properly send my resume by email.   1   2   3   4   5

57. Prepared to complete online profile forms in lieu
of my resume.   1   2   3   4   5

58. Considered the pros and cons of creating online
and video resumes.   1   2   3   4   5

59. Resume accompanied by an effective cover letter.   1   2   3   4   5

60. Only enclosed a cover letter with my
resume – nothing else.   1   2   3   4   5

61. Addressed letter to a specific name and position.   1   2   3   4   5

62. Mailed resume and cover letter in a matching
No. 10 business envelope or in a 9 x 12" envelope.   1   2   3   4   5

63. Typed address on envelope.   1   2   3   4   5

64. Sent correspondence by first-class or priority
mail or special next-day services; affixed
attractive commemorative stamps.   1   2   3   4   5

65. Considered pros and cons of faxing and/or
emailing resume to prospective employers.   1   2   3   4   5

FOLLOW-UP

66. Followed up the mailed resume within seven days.   1   2   3   4   5

67. Used the telephone to follow up.   1   2   3   4   5

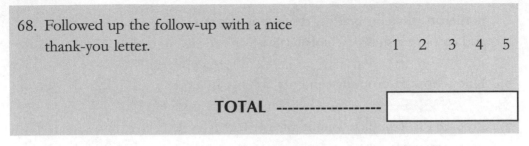

Add the numbers you circled to the right of each statement to get a total score. If your score is higher than 100, you need to work on improving your resume. Go back and make the necessary changes to create a truly dynamite resume.

External Resume Evaluation

In many respects the external resume evaluation plays the most crucial role in your overall job search. It helps you get remembered which, in turn, leads to referrals and job leads.

The best way to conduct an external evaluation is to circulate your resume to two or more individuals. Choose people whose opinions you value for being objective, frank, and thoughtful. Do not select friends and relatives who might flatter you with positive comments. Professional acquaintances or people you don't know personally but whom you admire may be good candidates for this type of evaluation.

An ideal evaluator has experience in hiring people in your area of expertise. In addition to sharing their experience with you, they may refer you to other individuals who would be interested in your qualifications. You will encounter many of these individuals in the process of networking and conducting informational interviews. You, in effect, conduct an external evaluation of your resume with the individual during the informational interview. At the very end of the informational interview you should ask the person to examine your resume; you want to find out how you can better strengthen the resume. Ask him or her the following questions:

"If you don't mind, would you look over my resume? Perhaps you could comment on its clarity or make suggestions for improving it?"

"How would you react to this resume if you received it from a candidate? Does it grab your attention and interest you enough to talk with me?"

"If you were writing this resume, what changes would you make? Any additions, deletions, or modifications?"

Answers to these questions should give you valuable feedback for improving both the form and content of your resume. You will be getting advice from people whose opinions count. However, it is not necessary to incorporate all such advice. Some evaluators, while well-meaning, will not provide you with sound advice, so take it all "with a grain of salt."

Another way to conduct an external evaluation is to develop a checklist of evaluation criteria and give it, along with your resume, to individuals whose opinions and expertise you value. Unlike the criteria used for the internal evaluation, the criteria for the external evaluation should be more general. Examine your resume in relation to these criteria:

Circle the number that best characterizes various aspects of my resume as well as include any recommendations on how I can best improve the resume:

1 = Excellent
2 = Okay
3 = Weak

				Recommendations for improvement
1. Overall appearance	1	2	3	_____
2. Layout	1	2	3	_____
3. Clarity	1	2	3	_____
4. Consistency	1	2	3	_____

5. Readability   1   2   3   _____

6. Language   1   2   3   _____

7. Organization   1   2   3   _____

8. Content/completeness   1   2   3   _____

9. Length   1   2   3   _____

10. Contact information/
    header   1   2   3   _____

11. Objective   1   2   3   _____

12. Experience   1   2   3   _____

13. Skills   1   2   3   _____

14. Achievements   1   2   3   _____

15. Education   1   2   3   _____

16. Other information   1   2   3   _____

17. Paper color   1   2   3   _____

18. Paper size and stock   1   2   3   _____

19. Overall production quality 1 2   3   _____

20. Potential effectiveness   1   2   3   _____

Summary Evaluation:

_____

_____

_____

_____

_____

_____

After you comple the external evaluation and incorporate useful suggestions for further improving the quality of your resume, it's a good idea to send a copy of your revised resume to those individuals who were helpful in giving you advice. Thank them for their time and thoughtful comments. Ask them to keep you in mind should they hear of anyone who might be interested in your experience and skills. In so doing, you will be demonstrating your appreciation and thoughtfulness as well as reminding them to remember you for further information, advice, and referrals.

In the end, **being remembered in reference to your resume** is one of the most important goals you want to repeatedly achieve during your job search. As you will quickly discover, your most effective job search strategy involves networking with your resume. You want to share information, by way of the networking conversations and informational interviews, about your interests and qualifications with those who can give advice, know about job vacancies, or can refer you to individuals who have the power to hire. Your resume, and especially this external evaluation, play a critical role in furthering this process.

Internal Letter Evaluation

Once you complete your first job search letter, conduct a thorough internal evaluation based upon the following criteria. Several of these criteria already appeared in previous chapters. They relate to each step in the letter writing process — structure, organization, production, distribution, and follow-up activities. Respond to each statement by circling the appropriate number to the right that most accurately describes your letter.

	Yes	Maybe	No

AUDIENCE

1. I know the needs of my audience based
   on my research of both the organization
   and the individual.   1   2   3

2. My letter clearly reflects an understanding
   of the needs of the organization and the
   letter recipient.   1   2   3

3. The letter recipient will remember me
   favorably based on the unique style
   and content of my letter.   1   2   3

4. My letter speaks the language of the
   employer – goals and benefits.   1   2   3

FORM, STRUCTURE, AND DESIGN

5. Makes an immediately good impression and
   is inviting to read.   1   2   3

6. First seven elements in letter (heading, date line,
   inside address, salutation, body, closing, signature
   lines) are present and adhere to the rules.   1   2   3

7. Body subdivided into 2-4 paragraphs.   1   2   3

8. Most paragraphs run no more than 5 lines.   1   2   3

9. Most sentences are 20 words or fewer in length. 1   2   3

10. Includes complete name and address
    of letter recipient.   1   2   3

11. Signed name looks strong and confident using a fountain or ballpoint pen.	1	2	3
12. Selected a standard typestyle.	1	2	3
13. Has a clean, crisp, uncluttered, and professional look.	1	2	3
14. Has a 1¼" to 1½" margin around the top, bottom, and sides.	1	2	3
15. Confined to a single page.	1	2	3

ORGANIZATION AND CONTENT

16. Immediately grabs the reader's attention	1	2	3
17. Presents most important ideas first.	1	2	3
18. Information expressed concisely.	1	2	3
19. Relates to the reader's interests and needs.	1	2	3
20. Persuades the reader to take action.	1	2	3
21. Free of spelling, grammatical, and punctuation errors.	1	2	3
22. Incorporates the active voice.	1	2	3
23. Avoids negative words and tone; uses positive language throughout.	1	2	3
24. Expresses the "unique you."	1	2	3
25. Employer-centered rather than self-centered.	1	2	3

26. Stresses benefits the reader is likely to
    receive from the letter writer.   1   2   3

27. Demonstrates a clear purpose.   1   2   3

28. Sentences and paragraphs flow logically.   1   2   3

29. Includes complete contact information
    (no P.O. Box numbers).   1   2   3

30. Expresses enthusiasm, energy, and fire.   1   2   3

31. Follows the ABC's of good writing (**A**lways
    Being **C**lear, **C**orrect, **C**omplete, **C**oncise,
    Courteous, **C**reative, **C**heerful, and **C**areful).   1   2   3

PRODUCTION QUALITY

32. Has an overall strong professional
    appearance sufficient to make an
    immediate favorable impression.   1   2   3

33. Adjusted copy setting properly – not
    too dark, not too light.   1   2   3

34. Type appears neat, clean, and straight.   1   2   3

35. Printed with a standard type style and size.   1   2   3

36. Produced on a letter-quality machine.   1   2   3

37. Proofread and ran spell-check (if using
    a word-processing program) for possible
    spelling/typing errors.   1   2   3

38. Used good quality paper stock that both
    looks and feels professional.   1   2   3

39. Selected a paper color appropriate
    for my audience.   1   2   3

40. Compared to nine other business letters
    received over the past year, this is
    one of three best in appearance.   1   2   3

DISTRIBUTION

41. Addressed to a specific name.   1   2   3

42. Used a No. 10 business or a 9 x 12"
    envelope.   1   2   3

43. Checked to make sure all enclosures
    got enclosed.   1   2   3

44. Matched the envelope paper stock and
    color to the stationery.   1   2   3

45. Typed the address and return address.   1   2   3

46. Affixed a commemorative stamp.   1   2   3

47. Used a special delivery service for
    overnight delivery.   1   2   3

48. Followed up letter immediately with
    a phone call.   1   2   3

FOLLOW-UP ACTIONS

49. Ended my letter with an action statement
    indicating I would contact the individual
    by phone within the next week.   1   2   3

50. Made the first follow-up call at the time
    and date indicated in my letter.   1   2   3

51. Followed up with additional phone calls until
    I was able to speak directly with the person or
    received the requested information.   1   2   3

52. Maintained a positive and professional
    attitude during each follow-up activity.
    Was pleasantly persistent and tactful
    during all follow-up calls. Never indicated
    I was irritated, insulted, or disappointed
    in not having my phone calls returned.   1   2   3

53. Followed up the follow-up by sending
    a thank-you letter genuinely expressing
    my appreciation for the person's time and
    information.   1   2   3

TOTAL ----------- [   ]

Add the numbers you circled to the right of each statement to get a cumulative score. If your score is higher than 60, you need to work on improving your letter effectiveness. Go back and make the necessary changes to create a dynamite letter.

External Letter Evaluation

You can best conduct an external evaluation of your letters by circulating them to two or more individuals. Choose people whose opinions are objective, frank, and thoughtful. Do not select friends and relatives who usually flatter you with positive comments. Professional acquaintances or people you don't know personally but whom you admire may be good evaluators. An ideal evaluator has had experience in hiring people in your area of job interest. In addition to sharing their experience with you, they may refer you to other individuals who would be interested in your qualifications. If you choose such individuals to critique both your letter and resume, ask them for their frank reaction – not what they would politely say to a candidate sending these materials. You want them to role play with you, an interview candidate. Ask your evaluators:

> ▪ *"How would you react to this letter if you received it from a candidate? Does it grab your attention and interest you enough to talk with me?"*

> ▪ *"If you were writing this letter, what changes would you make? Any additions, deletions, or modifications?"*

You should receive good advice and strong cooperation by approaching people for this external evaluation. In addition, you will probably get valuable unsolicited advice on other job search matters, such as job leads, job market information, and employment strategies.

Let your reader give you as much information as possible on the quality and potential impact of your letter. Taken together, the internal and external evaluations should complement each other and provide you with maximum useful information.

Appendix A

Resume Writing Worksheets

THE FOLLOWING WORKSHEETS are designed to help you capture all of the information about yourself that you'll need in order to write your resume. You'll want to make extra copies of some of the forms (e.g., Employment Experience Worksheet) so that you will have enough for each of your jobs. In this section you'll find:

- Employment Experience Worksheet
- Training and Education Worksheet
- Military Experience Worksheet
- Volunteer Experience Worksheet
- Skills and Special Qualifications Worksheet

We have created these worksheets so that any job seeker can use them – from mechanic to vice president. As such, there may be questions on the worksheets that do not apply to you or your particular situation. If so, just ignore them and move on to the next question. Be as thorough as possible, for the more information you generate about yourself, the more information you can pull from when you sit down to write your actual resume.

If you take the time to document all the information about yourself, you will find that the actual resume writing process moves along more easily and much faster. What's more, you'll also discover that your resume is better – it includes better information, it better highlights your skills and qualifications, it looks better, and it better represents "who" you are and "what" you can do. Simply put, it's a more effective job search tool that should help you in generating an employer's interest and capturing interviews.

Employment Experience Worksheet

1. Name of employer: _____

2. Address: _____

3. Dates of employment: from _____ to _____
                                   (month/year)   (month/year)

4. Job title:_____

5. Type of company: _____

6. Salary:_____

7. Responsibilities/duties:_____

    _____

    _____

    _____

    _____

8. Achievements: _____

    _____

    _____

    _____

    _____

9. Demonstrated skills:_____

    _____

    _____

    _____

    _____

Training and Education Worksheet

1. College degree and/or major: _____

2. College:_____

3. Address:_____

4. Dates: from _____ to _____   GPA: _____ (on _____ scale)

5. Honors and activities:_____

   _____

   _____

6. Certificate or license:_____

   _____

   _____

7. Company or organization:_____

   _____

   _____

8. Address: _____

   _____

9. Dates: from _____ to _____

10. Training program:_____

11. Company: _____

12. Address: _____

   _____

   _____

13. Dates: from _____ to _____

Military Experience Worksheet

1. Service:_____

2. Rank:_____

3. Inclusive dates: from _____ to _____.
   (month/year)   (month/year)

4. Responsibilities/duties: _____
   _____
   _____
   _____
   _____

5. Significant contributions/achievements: _____
   _____
   _____
   _____
   _____

6. Demonstrated skills and abilities:_____
   _____
   _____
   _____
   _____

7. Reserve status: _____

Volunteer Experience Worksheet

1. Name and address of organization/group:

   _____

   _____

   _____

2. Dates: from _____ to _____.
   (month/year)   (month/year)

3. Offices held/nature of involvement: _____

   _____

   _____

   _____

   _____

   _____

5. Significant contributions/achievements: _____

   _____

   _____

   _____

   _____

6. Demonstrated skills and abilities:_____

   _____

   _____

   _____

   _____

Skills and Special Qualifications Worksheet

1. Professional and community memberships:

   a._____

   b._____

   c._____

   d._____

2. Licenses and certifications:

   a._____

   b._____

   c._____

   d._____

3. Foreign languages and degree of competency:

   a._____

   b._____

4. Special awards and recognition:

   a._____

   b._____

   c._____

   d._____

5. Special skills, qualifications, and talents: _____

   _____

   _____

   _____

6. Interests, hobbies, and activities:

   a._____

   b._____

   c._____

   d._____

Appendix B

Action Verbs

FOLLOWING IS AN EXTENSIVE LIST of action verbs that you can use when writing your resumes, cover letters, thank-you letters, and other job search communications. Choose these words wisely and only use the words that accurately reflect your skills, capabilities, and work experience.

Accelerate	Assess	Compel
Accomplish	Assist	Compile
Achieve	Authorize	Complete
Acquire	Brief	Compute
Adapt	Build	Conceive
Address	Calculate	Conclude
Advance	Capture	Conduct
Advise	Catalog	Conserve
Advocate	Clarify	Consolidate
Analyze	Classify	Construct
Apply	Close	Consult
Appoint	Coach	Continue
Arbitrate	Collect	Contract
Arrange	Command	Convert
Ascertain	Communicate	Coordinate
Assemble	Compare	Correct

Counsel	Enhance	Inspire
Craft	Enlist	Install
Create	Ensure	Institute
Critique	Establish	Instruct
Decrease	Estimate	Integrate
Define	Evaluate	Intensify
Delegate	Examine	Interpret
Deliver	Exceed	Interview
Demonstrate	Execute	Introduce
Deploy	Exhibit	Invent
Design	Expand	Inventory
Detail	Expedite	Investigate
Detect	Experiment	Judge
Determine	Export	Justify
Develop	Facilitate	Launch
Devise	Finalize	Lead
Direct	Finance	Lecture
Discover	Form	Listen
Dispense	Formalize	Locate
Display	Formulate	Maintain
Distribute	Generate	Manage
Diversify	Govern	Manipulate
Divert	Guide	Manufacture
Document	Hire	Market
Draft	Hypothesize	Mastermind
Drive	Identify	Measure
Earn	Illustrate	Mediate
Edit	Imagine	Mentor
Educate	Implement	Model
Effect	Import	Modify
Elect	Improve	Monitor
Eliminate	Improvise	Motivate
Emphasize	Increase	Navigate
Enact	Influence	Negotiate
Encourage	Inform	Nominate
Endure	Initiate	Observe
Energize	Innovate	Obtain
Enforce	Inspect	Offer

Officiate	Receive	Standardize
Operate	Recognize	Stimulate
Orchestrate	Recommend	Streamline
Organize	Reconcile	Structure
Orient	Record	Succeed
Originate	Recruit	Suggest
Outsource	Redesign	Summarize
Overcome	Reduce	Supervise
Oversee	Regain	Supply
Participate	Regulate	Support
Perceive	Rehabilitate	Surpass
Perform	Reinforce	Synthesize
Persuade	Rejuvenate	Tabulate
Pinpoint	Render	Target
Pioneer	Renegotiate	Teach
Plan	Reorganize	Terminate
Position	Report	Test
Predict	Reposition	Train
Prepare	Represent	Transcribe
Prescribe	Research	Transfer
Present	Resolve	Transform
Preside	Respond	Transition
Process	Restore	Translate
Procure	Restructure	Troubleshoot
Program	Retrieve	Unify
Progress	Review	Unite
Project	Revise	Update
Promote	Revitalize	Upgrade
Propose	Satisfy	Use
Prospect	Schedule	Utilize
Provide	Select	Verbalize
Publicize	Sell	Verify
Purchase	Serve	Win
Qualify	Simplify	Write
Rate	Solidify	
Realign	Solve	
Rebuild	Speak	
Recapture	Specify	

Appendix C

Personality Descriptors

F ollowing is an extensive list of personality descriptors and characteristics that you can use when writing your resumes, cover letters, thank-
you letters, and other job search communications. Choose these words
wisely and only use the words that accurately reflect you, your personality, and
your talents.

Abstract	Competitive	Determined
Accurate	Conceptual	Devoted
Action-Driven	Confident	Diligent
Adaptable	Conscientious	Diplomatic
Adventuresome	Conservative	Direct
Aggressive	Cooperative	Dramatic
Amenable	Courageous	Driven
Analytical	Creative	Dynamic
Assertive	Credible	Eager
Believable	Cross-Cultural	Earnest
Bilingual	Culturally-Sensitive	Effective
Bold	Customer-Driven	Efficient
Brave	Decisive	Eloquent
Communicative	Dedicated	Employee-Driven
Competent	Dependable	Empowered

Encouraging	Keen	Proactive
Energetic	Leader	Problem-Solver
Energized	Loyal	Productive
Enterprising	Managerial	Professional
Enthusiastic	Market-Driven	Proficient
Entrepreneurial	Mature	Progressive
Ethical	Mechanical	Prominent
Experienced	Methodical	Prudent
Expert	Modern	Punctual
Expressive	Moral	Quality-Driven
Forward-Thinking	Motivated	Reactive
Global	Motivational	Reliable
Hardworking	Multilingual	Reputable
Healthy	Notable	Resilient
Helpful	Noteworthy	Resourceful
Heroic	Objective	Results-Driven
High-Impact	Observant	Results-Oriented
High-Potential	Opportunistic	Savvy
Honest	Orderly	Sensitive
Honorable	Organized	Sharp
Humanistic	Outstanding	Skilled
Humanitarian	Perfectionist	Skillful
Humorous	Performance-Driven	Sophisticated
Immediate	Persevering	Spirited
Impactful	Persistent	Strategic
Important	Personable	Strong
Impressive	Persuasive	Subjective
Incomparable	Philosophical	Successful
Independent	Photogenic	Tactful
Individualistic	Pioneering	Talented
Industrious	Poised	Team Builder
Ingenious	Polished	Team Leader
Innovative	Popular	Team Player
Insightful	Positive	Technical
Intelligent	Practical	Tenacious
Intense	Pragmatic	Thorough
Intuitive	Precise	Tolerant
Judicious	Prepared	Traditional

Trouble Shooter
Trustworthy
Truthful
Understanding
Unrelenting
Upbeat
Valuable
Verbal
Virtuous
Visionary
Vital
Vivacious
Well-Balanced
Well-Versed
Winning
Wise
Worldly
Youthful
Zealous

Transition Assistance for Ex-Offenders

The previous chapters and appendices outlined how you can write, produce, distribute, and follow up resumes and letters on your own. However, as hard as you may try, you may need assistance in writing your resumes and letters as well as completing other steps in your job search. Whatever you do, don't be afraid to ask for help. Indeed, you'll be pleasantly surprised to discover how many individuals and organizations are willing to help you with your transition. But you first need to know who they are and how to contact them for assistance.

Getting Help in Communities of Hope

Who will help you with your re-entry, especially with finding a job? Will you be on your own or will you be working with various support groups? Where will you initially look to for assistance in your community?

Once you've been released, chances are you will return to your former community where you will seek employment along with food, housing, transportation, credit, health care, and other necessities of life. You will probably re-unite with many friends, relatives, and acquaintances, including former employers. If you are on parole or probation, the terms of your release may require that you become documented, live and work in one community, regularly see your P.O., disclose your criminal history to employers, and avoid certain jobs because of your background.

If you're lucky, you may be quickly hired by a former employer or land a job through a family connection or referral from a friend. In fact, these are the best sources for finding a job, regardless of your background – informal, word-of-mouth contacts that also screen you for employment and thus help you deal with the troubling issue of disclosure.

However, not everyone is fortunate to have great personal connections to quickly find a job. Many ex-offenders, who soon exhaust their meager gate money, are in a scary survival mode – they need to get a job **now** just to pay for basic food, housing, and transportation. Some end up in homeless shelters or other types of transitional housing from which it may be difficult to conduct a job search. If this is your stituation, you especially need to follow the advice outlined in this appendix.

The first thing you need to do is understand various community safety nets designed to assist ex-offenders in transition. A community is more than just a place of opportunities to fulfill your dreams. It's made up of many individuals, groups, organizations, institutions, and neighborhoods that come together for achieving different goals. As they compete, cooperate, come into conflict, and co-op one another, they provide **opportunity structures** for finding jobs through informal, word-of-mouth channels.

The larger the community, the more safety nets and opportunity networks will be available to you. For example, the safety nets for ex-offenders in Chicago, Houston, New York City, Baltimore, and Washington, DC are much greater than in Sioux Falls, South Dakota, or Grand Prairie, Texas. However, the opportunity networks may be fewer in large poor cities that have high unemployment rates than in smaller cities and suburbs that have booming economies with very low unemployment.

Key Community Players for Ex-Offenders

Let's outline the key community players who can provide both a safety net and job opportunities for ex-offenders. They generally fall into these categories:

- **Government agencies and programs:** Social services, public health, courts, P.O.s, halfway houses, and One-Stop Career Centers.

- **Nonprofit and volunteer organizations:** Substance abuse centers, housing groups, public health groups, mental health organizations, legal services, and education and training organizations. Among the most prominent such organizations that regularly work with ex-offenders are Goodwill Industries and the Salvation Army.

- **Churches and other faith-based organizations:** Includes a wide range of denominations that offer everything from evangelical to social services as well as faith-based organizations involved in the federal government's new Ready4Work Prisoner Reentry Initiative jointly funded by the U.S. Department of Labor (Center for Faith-Based and Community Initiatives), the U.S. Department of Justice, and a consortium of private foundations.

A good way to look at communities is to visualize the safety nets and opportunity networks relating to you as found in the diagram on page 252.

Let's take, for example, the city of Baltimore, Maryland. Each year nearly 9,000 ex-offenders are released into this city. Like ex-offenders in many other large cities, nearly 80 percent in Baltimore move into the worst neighborhoods. Recognizing that both the city and ex-offenders face a major challenge, Baltimore has been very aggressive in dealing with the problem of ex-offenders becoming re-offenders by pulling together major community resources for dealing with the re-entry issue.

The Mayor's Office of Employment Development facilitated the creation of the Baltimore Citywide Ex-Offender Task Force in October 2002 to focus on ex-offender re-entry issues (www.oedworks.com/exoffender.htm). The Task Force included more than 100 government agencies and community partners. In March 2004, the Task Force was succeeded by a mayoral-appointed Ex-Offender Employment Steering Committee. Many of these agencies and organizations function as safety nets and opportunity networks for individuals who are unemployed, homeless, hungry, sick, victims of domestic violence, mentally ill, HIV/AIDS infected, or substance abusers. Examples of such service providers include:

EMPLOYMENT

- Baltimore Works One-Stop Career Center
- Career Development and Cooperative Education Center
- Caroline Center
- Damascus Career Center
- Goodwill Industries of the Chesapeake

- Maryland New Directions
- Prisoners Aid Association of Maryland, Inc.

HEALTH

- First Call for Help
- Health Care for the Homeless
- Jai Medical Center
- Maryland Youth Crisis Hotline
- Rape Crisis Center
- Sisters Together and Reaching, Inc.
- The Men's Health Center
- Black Educational AIDS Project

HOUSING

- 20th Street Hope House
- AIDS Interfaith Residential Services
- At Jacob's Well
- Baltimore Rescue Mission
- Cottage Avenue Community Transitional Housing
- Helping Up Mission
- Light Street Housing
- Maryland Re-Entry Program
- Safe Haven
- Salvation Army

LEGAL

- Homeless Persons Representation Project
- House of Ruth, Domestic Violence Legal Clinic
- Lawyer Referral & Information Service
- Legal Aid Bureau
- Office of the Public Defender
- University of Baltimore School of Law

MENTAL HEALTH

- Baltimore Crisis Response Center
- Department of Social Services

- Family Help Line
- Gamblers Anonymous
- North Baltimore Center
- People Encouraging People
- Suicide Prevention Hotline
- You Are Never Alone

SUBSTANCE ABUSE

- Bright Hope House
- I Can't, We Can, Inc.
- Addict Referral and Counseling Center
- Crossroads Center
- Day Break Rehabilitation Program
- Friendship House
- SAFE House

FOOD AND CLOTHING

- Salvation Army
- Bethel Outreach Center, Inc.
- Our Daily Bread
- Paul's Place

Baltimore has also initiated a transitional jobs project, Project Bridge, for ex-offenders. It's a collaborative effort involving Goodwill Industries of the Chesapeake; Associated Catholic Charities; the Center for Fathers, Families, and Workforce Development; and the Second Chance Project. Targeted toward ex-offenders who are unlikely to find employment on their own, the project provides eligible ex-offenders returning to Baltimore with transitional employment, support services, and job placement, followed by 12 months of post-placement retention services.

Community Resources

Many large communities, especially New York City, Chicago, Detroit, Houston, Los Angeles, and Washington, DC, offer various types of assistance programs for ex-offenders. If you have Internet access, you can quickly locate such programs and services in your community. For an excellent summary of government agencies and community-based organizations assisting ex-offenders with employment, legal, and other re-entry issues, including referrals to other relevant organizations, be sure to visit the National H.I.R.E. Network Website, which is an information clearinghouse that provides access to resources in all 50 states:

www.hirenetwork.org/resource.html

Other useful websites include:

GOVERNMENT

- Center for Employment Opportunities (New York City)   www.CEOworks.org
- Federal Bureau of Prisons   www.bop.gov
- U.S. Parole Commission   www.usdoj.gov/uspc/parole.htm
- U.S. Office of Justice Programs   www.ojp.usdoj.gov/reentry
- U.S. Department of Labor, Center for Faith-Based and Community Initiatives   www.dol-tlc.org
- Volunteers of America   www.voa.org

ASSOCIATIONS

- American Correctional Association   www.aca.org
- American Jail Association   www.corrections.com/aja
- Corrections Connection   www.corrections.com

NONPROFIT/VOLUNTEER

- The Safer Foundation   www.saferfoundation.org
- OPEN, INC.   www.openinc.org
- Just The Necessities   www.justthenecessities.org
- The Sentencing Project   www.sentencingproject.org
- Family and Corrections Network   www.fcnetwork.org
- Legal Action Center   www.lac.org
- Criminal Justice Policy Foundation   www.cjpf.org/clemency/ clemency.html

- Annie E. Casey Foundation   www.aecf.org
- The Fortune Society   www.fortunesociety.org
- Second Chance/STRIVE (San Diego)   www.secondchanceprogram.org

FAITH-BASED

- Prison Fellowship Ministries — www.pfm.org
- Re-Entry Prison and Jail Ministry — www.reentry.org/cgi-bin/resource.cfm
- Conquest Offender Reintegration Ministries (Washington, DC) — www.conquesthouse.org/links.html
- Breakthrough Urban Ministries (Chicago) — www.breakthroughministries.com
- Exodus Transitional Community, Inc. (New York) — www.etcny.org
- Transition of Prisoners, Inc. — www.topinc.net
- Work Ministry — www.workministry.com

These and other useful resources can be quickly accessed through the "Useful Links" section on our companion ex-offender re-entry website:

www.ExoffenderReentry.com

Identifying Your Community Resources

What is different among communities is the degree to which a community actually recognizes the need to focus on ex-offender re-entry issues. If you enter a community that does not provide specific assistance and services to ex-offenders, you'll be on your own in a sea of government agencies and community-based organizations that primarily provide employment and safety net services for disadvantaged groups, similar to the ones we identified on pages 247-249. Therefore, one of your most important initial jobs will be to understand how your particular community is structured in terms of such networks and relationships. You want to put specific names on the various categories of organizations we outlined in the figure on page 252. Once you understand your community, you should be prepared to take advantage of the many services and opportunities available to someone in your situation.

You can start identifying your community networks by completing the following exercise. Specify the actual names of up to five different government agencies and community-based organizations for each category that you need to know about and possibly use in the coming weeks and months. Remember

Community Safety Nets and Opportunity Networks

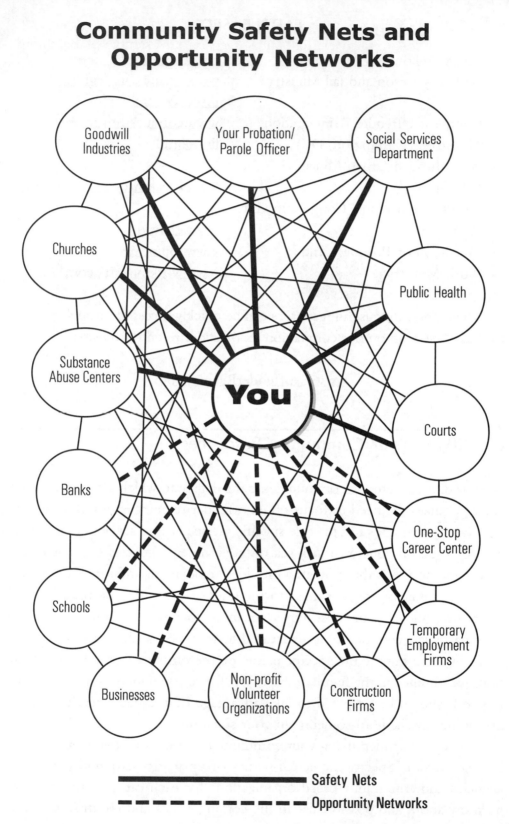

the three types of organizations we identified on pages 246-247 – government, nonprofit/volunteer, and church/faith-based in our example of Baltimore. If you don't have this information on your community, ask your P.O. for assistance, visit your local library and ask personnel at the information desk for assistance, do an Internet search, or contact your local government social services department.

Identify Your Community Safety Nets and Opportunity Networks

My target community: _____

Employment groups

1. _____
2. _____
3. _____
4. _____
5. _____

Housing groups

1. _____
2. _____
3. _____
4. _____
5. _____

Food and clothing groups

1. _____
2. _____
3. _____
4. _____
5. _____

Health care groups

1. _____
2. _____

3. _____

4. _____

5. _____

Mental health groups (if an issue)

1. _____

2. _____

3. _____

4. _____

5. _____

Substance abuse groups (if an issue)

1. _____

2. _____

3. _____

4. _____

5. _____

Legal groups

1. _____

2. _____

3. _____

4. _____

5. _____

Other groups

1. _____

2. _____

3. _____

4. _____

5. _____

The Importance of One-Stop Career Centers

One community group you should become familiar with is your local One-Stop Career Center. Indeed, make sure you visit a One-Stop Career Center soon after release. It may well become one of your most important lifelines for landing your first job out.

Usually operated by the state employment office, One-Stop Career Centers provide numerous resources for assisting individuals in finding employment, such as computerized job banks, job listings, counseling and assessment services, job search assistance, and training programs. They also may provide resume and letter writing assistance. Since career professionals staffing these centers increasingly work with ex-offenders, you'll be no stranger to their offices. Be sure to disclose your background to their personnel, since knowing about your criminal record may result in special contacts and services. The personnel in many of the centers regularly work with ex-offenders and know ex-offender-friendly employers. In fact, you may find one staff member whose job is to work specifically with ex-offenders. You can easily find the center nearest you by visiting this website:

- **One-Stop Career Centers**　　　<u>www.careeronestop.org</u>

You'll also want to visit these two related websites operated by the U.S. Department of Labor:

- **America's CareerInfoNet**　　　<u>www.acinet.org</u>
- **America's Service Locator**　　　<u>www.servicelocator.org</u>

Consider Using Temporary Employment Agencies

You also may want to contact various temporary employment agencies or staffing firms. This is good way to quickly get employed and acquire work experience. With temporary employment agencies, you work for the agency, which, in turn, places you on temporary assignments with its clients. While these companies primarily recruit individuals for temporary or part-time positions, many of these firms also have temp-to-perm programs. With these programs, you may work two to three months with one employer who may decide to hire you full-time once your contract expires with the temporary employment agency if you have met their performance expectations. Many large cities have over 200 such firms operating. Many of these agencies specialize in particular occupations, such as construction, accounting, information technology, law, and health care services. Other agencies may recruit for all types of positions, including many low-skill, low-wage labor positions. Some of the most popular temporary employment agencies with a nationwide presence include:

- **Labor Finders**   www.laborfinders.com
- **Manpower**   www.manpower.com
- **Olsten**   www.olsten.com
- **Kelly Services**   www.kellyservices.com

Working With a Professional

Many ex-offenders face difficulties in writing, producing, and distributing resumes and letters. Most of these difficulties center on some or all of the following:

- Limited or unstable work history
- Low levels of education and training
- Unclear goals and lack of focus
- Weak organization and writing skills
- An "experience" time gap while incarcerated
- Uncertainty about marketing oneself
- Lack of equipment and money for production and distribution

In other words, ex-offenders are likely to make many of the mistakes we outlined in previous chapters. If these difficulties characterize your situation, and you are not a talented writer, by all means seek assistance in writing your resume and letters. Don't pretend you can write and distribute on your own by just following our advice. It simply won't happen, or the product will be third-rate.

A career professional can give you much-needed advice and assistance in putting together a resume that best represents you and is targeted toward the right people. Hopefully you will participate in a pre-release program that assists you in writing a resume. If not, once you are released, contact a local support group, participate in a job readiness program, or contact personnel at your local One-Stop Career Center for assistance in writing a resume. You also can hire a professional resume writer to develop your resume. Most will charge you from $200 to $600 for their services. If you can afford such a professional, they will probably produce an outstanding resume that will grab the attention of employers as well as help you focus your job search. In addition to consulting the professionals who contributed to this book (see Appendix E), you can contact professional resume writers through these organizations:

- **Career Masters Institute**   www.cminstitute.com
- **National Resume Writers' Association**   www.nrwaweb.com
- **Professional Association of Resume Writers and Career Coaches**   www.parw.com
- **Professional Resume Writing and Research Association**   www.prwra.com

You can see some terrific examples of their work by reviewing the following resume books written by professional resume writers, which are available in many libraries or through Impact Publications (www.impactpublications.com):

- *101 Best Resumes*
- *101 More Best Resumes*
- *202 Great Resumes*
- *Best Career Transition Resumes for $100,000+ Jobs*
- *Best Cover Letters for $100,000+ Jobs*
- *Best KeyWords for Resumes, Cover Letters, and Interviews*
- *Best Resumes for $100,000+ Jobs*
- *Best Resumes for People Without a Four-Year Degree*
- *Blue Collar Resumes*
- *The Damn Good Resume Guide*
- *Executive Job Search for $100,000 to $1 Million+ Jobs*
- *Expert Resumes for Career Changers*
- *Expert Resumes for Computer and Web Jobs*
- *Expert Resumes for Manufacturing Careers*
- *Expert Resumes for People Returning to Work*
- *Gallery of Best Resumes for People Without a Four-Year Degree*
- *The Resume Catalog*
- *Resume Magic*
- *Resumes That Knock 'Em Dead*

Indeed, you can learn a great deal about resumes for particular occupations by examining the many resume examples in these books.

For step-by-step instructions on how to produce each section of your resume as well as information on production, distribution, and follow-up, see three of our other books:

- *High Impact Resumes and Letters*
- *Nail the Resume!*
- *The Savvy Resume Writer*

We also highly recommend Joyce Lain Kennedy's terrific book on resume writing:

- *Resumes for Dummies*

Used together with our book, these resume writing and example books will give you sufficient information to create your own winning resume.

E List of Contributors

FOLLOWING ARE ALL OF THE RESUME writers, career coaches, career counselors, transition assistance professionals, and other career experts who contributed their resumes and expertise to this book.

Michelle Angello, CPRW
Corbel Communications
19866 E. Dickenson Place
Aurora, CO 80013
303-537-3592
corbelcomm1@aol.com
www.corbelonline.com

Elizabeth Crimi, GCDF, OWDS, MBTI-Qualified
MD State Department of Education – Correctional Education
MD Correctional Institution for Women, Education Department
7943 Brock Bridge Road
Jessup, MD 20794
410-379-3830

Michael Davis, GCDF, CPRW
The Michaels Group
110 North Main St., Ste. 1280
Dayton, OH 45402
937-224-5281
msdavis49@hotmail.com

Louise Garver, CMP, CPRW, MCDP, CEIP, JCTC
Career Directions, LLC
143 Melrose Road
Broad Brook, CT 06016
860-623-9476
CareerPro@cox.net
www.resumeimpact.com

Lee Ann Grundish
Grafix Services / ACHIEVE SUCCESS!™
Toledo / Ottawa Hills, OH
419-534-2709 / 419-472-5989
GrafixServices@aol.com
www.grafixservices.com

Andrea Howard, M.S., Ed.
NYS Department of Labor
Career Central
175 Central Avenue
Albany, NY 12206
518-462-7600 x 124
usaah3@labor.state.ny.us
www.labor.state.ny.us

Veda Swift Jeffries, M.S.
Stanford University
Career Development Center
563 Salvatierra Walk
Stanford, CA 94305
650-725-2824
Veej@stanford.edu

Brian Leeson, M.Sc.
Vector Consultants Pty. Ltd.
P.O. Box 553
Echunga, South Australia, 5153
Australia
+61 8 8388 8183
vector@adelaide.on.net

Linda Martel, B.A.
Career Consultant / Coach
lindamartel@rogers.com

Ellen Mulqueen, CRW, M.A.
The Institute of Living
200 Retreat Avenue
Hartford, CT 06106
860-545-7202
emulque@harthosp.org
www.instituteofliving.org

William G. Murdock, CPRW
The Employment Coach
7770 Meadow Road, Suite 109
Dallas, TX 75230
214-750-4781
bmurdock@swbell.net
www.resumesinaction.com

Melanie Noonan, CPS
Peripheral Pro, LLC
560 Lackawanna Avenue
West Paterson, NJ 07424
973-785-3011
PeriPro1@aol.com

Constance Parker, M.S., OWDS
MD State Department of Education – Correctional Education
MD Correctional Institution for Women, Education Department
7943 Brock Bridge Road
Jessup, MD 20794
410-379-3830

Jane Roqueplot, CPBA, CWDP, CECC
JaneCo's Sensible Solutions
194 North Oakland Avenue
Sharon, PA 16146
888-526-3267
info@janecos.com
www.janecos.com

Teena Rose, CPRW, CEIP, CCM
Resume to Referral
1824 Rebert Pike
Springfield, OH 45506
937-325-2149
admin@resumetoreferral.com
www.resumebycprw.com

Janice Shepherd, CPRW, JCTC, CEIP
Write On Career Keys
2628 East Crestline Drive
Bellingham, WA 98226-4260
360-738-7958
Janice@writeoncareerkeys.com
www.writeoncareerkeys.com

Bob Simmons
Career Transition Associates
1670 Old Country Road, Suite 117
Plainview, NY 11803
516 -501-0717
bob@ctajobsearch.com
www.ctajobsearch.com

Gina Taylor, MRW, CPRW
A-1 Advantage Career Services
1111 W. 77th Terrace
Kansas City, MO 64114
816-523-9100
ginaresume@sbcglobal.net
ginataylor.com

Beth Woodworth, M.S.
Job Training Center of Tehama County
718 Main Street
Red Bluff, CA 96080
530-529-7000
bwoodworth@ncen.org
www.jobtrainingcenter.org

The Authors

WENDY S. ENELOW, CCM, MRW, JCTC, CPRW, is a recognized leader in the executive job search, career coaching, and resume writing industries. In private practice for nearly 25 years, she has assisted thousands of job search candidates through successful career transition. She also is the founder and former president of the Career Masters Institute, an exclusive training and development association for career professionals worldwide. The principal author of more than 25 career books, she has most recently written *Best Career Transition Resumes for $100,000+ Jobs, Expert Resumes for Career Changers, Expert Resumes for Military-to-Civilian Transitions, Expert Resumes for People Returning to Work, KeyWords to Nail Your Job Interview,* and *The $100,000+ Job Interview.* A graduate of the University of Maryland, Wendy has earned several distinguished professional credentials. She can be contacted through the publisher or at wendy@wendyenelow.com.

RONALD L. KRANNICH, Ph.D., is one of America's leading career and travel specialists with more than 3 million books in print. He is the principal author of more than 80 books, including such noted career titles as *The Ex-Offender's Job Hunting Guide, Job Interview Tips for People With Hot and Not-So-Hot Backgrounds, High Impact Resumes and Letters, Nail the Resume!, Nail the Cover Letter!, Nail the Job Interview!, I Want to Do Something Else But I'm Not Sure What It Is, Interview for Success, Dynamite Salary Negotiations, The Savvy Networker, Jobs for Travel Lovers,*

America's Top Internet Job Sites, and *Change Your Job, Change Your Life*. Ron is president of Development Concepts Incorporated, a training, consulting, and publishing firm in Virginia. A former Peace Corps Volunteer, high school teacher, university professor, and Fulbright Scholar, he received his Ph.D. in Political Science from Northern Illinois University. He can be contacted through the publisher or at krannich@impactpublications.com.

Job Hunting Kit
For People With Challenging Backgrounds

We're pleased to offer this unique collection of books dealing with important employability issues. Written by four of America's career experts, these books are designed to help people with not-so-hot backgrounds develop the necessary knowledge and skills to quickly land a job. Essential resources for every career library and resource center. Can purchase separately. SPECIAL: $99.95 for all 7 books.

Job Hunting Tips for People With Hot and Not-So-Hot Backgrounds
150 Smart Tips That Can Change Your Life
Ron and Caryl Krannich, Ph.Ds

Finding a job may be the hardest, most frustrating, and ego-bruising work you will ever do. Depending on how you approach the process, it can also be an extremely educational, exciting, and exhilarating experience. This unique book presents 150 job hunting tips that are applicable to most job seekers, regardless of their backgrounds. Organized around a step-by-step job search process, it includes tips on everything from conducting a self-assessment, developing an objective, and conducting research to completing applications, writing resumes and letters, networking, interviewing, and negotiating salary. 2005. 6 x 9. 240 pages. ISBN 1-57023-225-3. $17.95

America's Top Jobs for People Re-Entering the Workforce
Ron and Caryl Krannich, Ph.Ds

Reveals a wealth of job opportunities for individuals who are restarting a career, changing careers, or simply looking for work in areas that require limited direct work experience. Addresses specific jobs appropriate for re-entry groups, including homemakers, career changers, ex-offenders, military in transition, people with disabilities, students, and retirees. 2005. 6 x 9. 285 pages. ISBN 1-57023-226-1. $19.95

No One Will Hire Me! (2nd Ed.)
Ron and Caryl Krannich, Ph.Ds

It's the often-heard lament of the disillusioned job seeker – *"No one will hire me!"* Misunderstanding job market realities, job seekers make numerous mistakes that frequently result in self-fulfilling prophecies. Two of America's leading career experts identify 15 key mistakes job seekers make, from failing to articulate goals and knowing one's worth to improperly using Internet resources and prematurely accepting a job offer. Each chapter identifies a major mistake and then offers analyses, self-tests, exercises, and resources for avoiding the error in the future. The perfect job search guide for everyone, from students, job changers, and displaced executives to ex-offenders and transitioning military personnel. 2004. 6 x 9. 192 pages. ISBN 1-57023-219-9. $13.95

Nail the Job Interview!
Ron and Caryl Krannich, Ph.Ds

Shows how to apply 45 key principles to the job interview; develop winning answers; deal with personality, motivation, and education; turn negative questions into positive answers; communicate positive nonverbal messages; handle behavioral questions; ask 30 key questions about the job and the employer; and much more. 2003. 6 x 9. 192 pages. ISBN 1-57023-219-9. $13.95. Audio version $16.95. SPECIAL: Both book and audio for $29.95

Job Interview Tips for People With Not-So-Hot Backgrounds
Caryl and Ron Krannich, Ph.Ds

You must do well in the job interview to get a job offer. But what should you say and do if your background includes red flags – you've been incarcerated, got fired, received poor grades, or lack necessary skills? This book speaks to millions of individuals who have difficult but promising backgrounds. Shows how to best prepare for interview questions that could become job knock-outs. Filled with numerous examples and cases to illustrate how to provide honest and positive answers. 2004. 6 x 9. ISBN 1-57023-213-X. $14.95. *"A great value that belongs in every resource room and on the shelf of every career counselor or case manager who serves people with barriers to employability." – NAWDP Advantage*

95 Mistakes Job Seekers Make and How to Avoid Them
Richard Fein

Based on a survey of hundreds of seasoned employers, this unique book outlines 95 common mistakes many job seekers make as well as insightful remedies for each error. A great resource for developing an effective job search that responds to the needs of employers. Jam-packed with inside advice from employers and career experts. 2003. 6 x 9. 140 pages. ISBN 1-57023-198-2. $13.95

America's Top 100 Jobs for People Without a Four-Year Degree
Ron and Caryl Krannich, Ph.Ds

This book analyzes 100 jobs by employment outlook, nature of work, working conditions, education and training requirements, and earnings. It also includes key contact information on education and training opportunities, professional associations, and useful websites. 2005. 6 x 9. 285 pages. ISBN 1-57023-214-8. $19.95

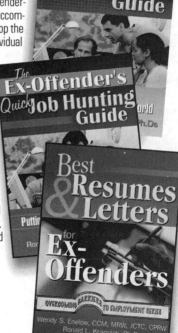

Stay Out for Good!
Job Finding Kit

Here's the ultimate collection of books designed to assist ex-offenders in finding jobs and staying out for good. Can purchase separately.

SPECIAL: $199.95 for complete set of 18 books (plus shipping).

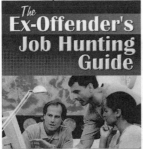

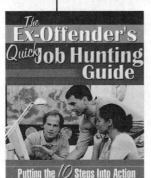

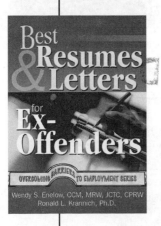

- *9 to 5 Beats Ten to Life* ($15.00)
- *99 Days and a Get Up* ($9.95)
- *America's Top 100 Jobs for People Without a Four-Year Degree* ($19.95)
- *America's Top Jobs for People Re-Entering the Workforce* ($19.95)
- *Best Resumes and Letters for Ex-Offenders* ($19.95)
- *The Ex-Offender's Job Hunting Guide* ($17.95)
- *Ex-Offender's Job Search Companion* ($11.95)
- *The Ex-Offender's Quick Job Hunting Guide* ($9.95)
- *Job Hunting Tips for People With Hot and Not-So-Hot Backgrounds* ($17.95)
- *Job Interview Tips for People With Not-So-Hot Backgrounds* ($14.95)
- *Man, I Need a Job* ($7.95)
- *No One Will Hire Me!* ($13.95)
- *Putting the Bars Behind You* (6 books, $57.95)

For information on these and other resources (videos, DVDs, software, posters, games, assessment instruments, special value kits, downloadable catalogs and flyers) relevant to ex-offenders and re-entry success, visit ***www.impactpublications.com***.

How to Order: Impact Publications, 9104-N Manasssas Drive, VA 20111, Tel. 1-800-361-1055, Fax 703-335-9486, or email: info@impactpublications.com.